Econometric Studies in Energy Demand and Supply

edited by
G. S. Maddala
Wen S. Chern
Gurmukh S. Gill

The Praeger Special Studies program,
through a selective worldwide distribution
network, makes available to the academic,
government, and business communities significant and timely research in U.S. and
international economic, social, and political issues.

Econometric Studies in Energy Demand and Supply

Praeger Publishers   New York   London

Library of Congress Cataloging in Publication Data

Main entry under title:

Econometric studies in energy demand and supply.

   Includes bibliographical references.
   1. Fuel trade--United States--Addresses, essays,
lectures. 2. Power resources--United States--
Mathematical models--Addresses, essays, lectures.
3. Electrical utilities--United States--Mathematical
models--Addresses, essays, lectures. I. Maddala,
G. S. II. Chern, Wen S. III. Gill, Gurmukh Singh, 1930-

HD9544. E27 1978   333.7   78-2886
ISBN 0-03-042266-3

PRAEGER SPECIAL STUDIES
200 Park Avenue, New York, N.Y., 10017, U.S.A.

Published in the United States of America in 1978
by Praeger Publishers,
A Division of Holt, Rinehart and Winston, CBS, Inc.

89   038   987654321

ACKNOWLEDGMENTS

Except for the study by R. Blaine Roberts, all the studies in this book were started while the editors were together in the energy division of the Oak Ridge National Laboratory during the summer of 1975. The research contained in these papers was supported by the National Science Foundation RANN program and the Energy Research and Development Administration (ERDA) under Union Carbide's contract with ERDA. The authors of these papers would like to thank Roger S. Carlsmith, under whose supervision these studies were conducted. In addition, Chern and Lin would like to acknowledge the helpful comments of E. Hirst of the Oak Ridge National Laboratory and D. A. Pilati of the University of Illinois. None of the foregoing agencies, institutions, or individuals is responsible for the opinions expressed in these studies or for any errors that remain.

We would also like to thank the following journals for permission to include in this volume papers that appeared in them: American Statistical Association: Proceedings of the Business and Economic Statistical Section 1975: papers appearing in Chapters 3, 4, and 8; and Journal of Environmental Economics and Management: paper appearing in Chapter 6.

CONTENTS

LIST OF TABLES

LIST OF FIGURES

Econometric Studies
in Energy Demand
and Supply

INTRODUCTION
G. S. Maddala

The chapters in this volume are not addressed to finding
"solutions" for our "energy problem" nor to the derivation of policy
implications for politicians to implement. They do have policy implications and these are discussed at the appropriate places. But
the basic concern in the chapters is to analyze carefully the relevant
data for the problem at hand without being too anxious to jump to un-
justified and hasty policy conclusions. The techniques of analysis
used are very broad and varied in nature (much more so than other
books in this area). They cover estimation of market share equations, logit models, linear programming models, switching regression models, variance components models, logistic growth curves,
and so on. It is thus hoped that this collection will be of some use
from the methodological point of view as well and will help other
investigators in their analyses of different problems in the area of
energy demand and supply. We will therefore discuss both the substantive and methodological aspects of each of these studies.

Chapter 2 by Wen S. Chern, "Aggregate Demand for Energy
in the United States," deals first with the residential and commercial sectors for which oil, natural gas, and electricity are considered. Coal was considered initially but was dropped later because
the price of coal was never significant in the share equations of
other fuels and prices of other fuels were not significant in the
share equation for coal. In any case the consumption of coal is of
minimal magnitude in the residential and commercial sectors. The
model consists of an aggregate demand equation and three share
equations explaining the relative shares of the three fuels in total
energy demand. From these Chern derives the conditional demand
elasticities (conditional on given aggregate demand) and the (conventional) unconditional demand elasticities. Next, assuming some
conversion factors for converting one energy type into another (for

example, natural gas to electricity), he derives price elasticities
for total end-use energy and "primary" energy. Raising the price
of any particular energy type will reduce the demand for that source
but will increase the demand for other types of energy due to interfuel substitution. In terms of end-use energy, Chern finds that raising petroleum prices (rather than the prices of natural gas and electricity) has the highest impact on aggregate demand for energy
(after allowing for interfuel substitution effects). On the other hand,
if we look at primary energy, raising electricity prices has the highest impact on aggregate demand. It is thus very important to distinguish between end-use energy and primary energy for policy purposes.

Apart from these substantive conclusions, there is some
methodological interest in the chapter. Instead of having separate
demand equations for the different fuel types, the study follows the
path of having an aggregate demand equation and share equations for
the different fuels. This "market-shares approach" is perhaps
more illuminating than the other approach, and in some cases it may
be the more appropriate one where time-series data are available to
estimate the aggregate demand equation but only cross-section data
are available to estimate the demand equations for the separate fuels.

Chern does not consider the transportation sector at all, and
for the case of industrial demand he considers only the demand for
electricity. Also, data limitations force him to combine different
industrial groups, though he does address himself to problems of
simultaneity between quantity and price. A lot more work needs to
be done in this area, particularly estimating demand functions for
different fuels and also estimating the demand functions by different
industry groups (rather than a cross-industry equation as estimated
by Chern).

Chapter 3 by Gurmukh S. Gill and G. S. Maddala, "Residential
Demand for Electricity in the TVA Area," analyzes that demand
during the 1962-72 period. The study is based on a time series of
11 years for 147 distributors. Apart from showing that there has
been a definite structural break in the demand function in 1967, the
chapter illustrates problems of analyzing structural change and in
pooling cross-section and time-series data using the variance components models and least squares with dummy variables.

Chapter 4 by Wen S. Chern and William W. Lin, "Energy Demand for Space Heating in the United States," breaks up the demand
for space heating into two components: the short-run usage function,
and the long-run fuel-choice function which characterizes the appliance ownership decision. The study finds that the usage elasticities
are much smaller than the appliance choice elasticities. On the
methodological side, the chapter illustrates the use of the market

shares approach (used in Chapter 2) and the estimation of logit models used in fuel choice functions.

Chapter 5 by Gurmukh S. Gill, G. S. Maddala, and Steve M. Cohn, "The Growth of Electric Heating in the TVA Area," analyzes the data (by distributors) considered in Chapter 3. The study is a very good illustrative example of the estimation of logistic growth curves and some pitfalls in their use, particularly when the growth process is still continuing and has not attained the ceiling. The study is a substantial improvement over earlier studies of Anderson and NERA (referred to in the paper) on the growth of electric heating. These studies implicitly assume that the ceiling proportion of electric heating will be 100 percent.

Chapter 6 by William W. Lin, "Appalachian Coal: Supply and Demand," is addressed to the estimation of the effects of strip-mining legislation on coal supply and mining employment in Appalachia. This study is a good illustration of the use of linear programming model and engineering data to derive supply functions. Lin finds that the economic impact of legislation is considerably smaller than the casual estimates which have previously been suggested by policy makers. This study therefore illustrates the importance of careful analysis of available data as an input to policy decision making.

Chapter 7 by R. Blaine Roberts, "Estimation of Optimal Inventory of Coal Stocks Held by Electric Utilities," tries to explain the wide fluctuations in inventories of coal stocks held by electric utilities. The chapter develops a theoretical model of cost minimization under uncertainty for electric utilities holding coal stocks. The model, interestingly enough, results in a switching regression model with endogenous switching. It is shown that the observed data points lie on the marginal cost curve or a constrained curve, depending on the value of a criterion function. Though the estimation of this switching model is theoretically possible, the available data precluded such an attempt and Roberts used the usual regression models (correcting for serial correlation in the residuals). He found the predictions obtained by these methods quite satisfactory.

Chapter 8 by Gurmukh S. Gill, "Omitted Cross-Sectional Effects in Measurement of Economies of Scale in Electricity Generation," stresses the important point (well-known but often unheeded) that one cannot get an idea of economies of scale from a pure cross-sectional analysis. During recent years more elaborate functional forms (like the translog cost function) have been used to study the problem of economies of scale, but the elaborate functional forms do not avoid the problem of omitted cross-sectional effects.

Chapter 9 by Michael A. Zimmer, "Empirical Tests of the Averch-Johnson Hypothesis: A Critical Appraisal," gives a survey of recent empirical work on the effect of regulation on capital utilization by electric utilities. In particular it argues that none of these studies have paid enough attention to the estimation of the cost of capital, which is a crucial variable in the analysis.

The chapters in this volume cover a broad variety of topics and techniques of analysis. It is not possible, in such a small volume, to attack all aspects of the energy problem. To do full justice to even a single source of energy--oil, natural gas, coal, or electricity--will take a volume much bigger than this one. The book does not have a chapter on gasoline, or the transportation sector. Nor does it have a model with 20 or 50 equations in it. Such models are no doubt the fashion nowadays (the bigger the better), but it is so easy to get lost in them and it is very difficult to see what is going on. The purpose in these studies is to work more intensely on specific sectors and equations. There is, however, greater emphasis on electricity than on the other sources of energy. Chapters 8 and 9 are concerned with electricity supply and Chapter 7 is on demand for coal by electric utilities. Chapters 3 and 5 are concerned with electricity demand (in the TVA area) and Chapters 2 and 4 also discuss, in addition to that for other fuels, the demand for electricity in the residential and commercial sectors. Chapter 6 is solely concerned with coal. To cure this imbalance would have necessitated the inclusion of many more chapters.

2

AGGREGATE DEMAND FOR
ENERGY IN THE
UNITED STATES
Wen S. Chern

Conversion of such energy sources as coal and nuclear power to electricity for end uses makes it necessary to distinguish end-use from primary energy. Electricity is an end-use energy source, but not a primary energy. On the other hand, nuclear power is seldomly used directly to satisfy the end-use demand; it is a primary energy source for electric generation. Natural gas, petroleum products, and coal are used directly for end uses and for electricity generation. Thus primary energy includes all energy sources being extracted, refined, and used directly for end uses and for electricity generation. End-use energy, on the other hand, refers to energy sources at points of end use. At the aggregate level, end-use consumption plus losses of energy in electric generation, transmission, and distribution constitute total demand for primary energy sources.

Historically, the U.S. consumption for energy grew at a very rapid rate. During the period 1961-73, prior to the oil embargo, consumption of energy sources at points of end use grew at a rate of 3.9 percent per year (Table 2.1). For total consumption of primary energy sources, the growth rate was 4.3 percent per year during this period. Demand dropped in 1974 and again in 1975; it increased slightly in 1976. As a result, the rates of growth in both total primary energy and end-use energy consumption dropped during the 1973-76 period. If one examines the historical trend of energy

Research sponsored by the National Science Foundation RANN Program and the U.S. Energy Research and Development Administration under contract with the Union Carbide Corporation, Oak Ridge National Laboratory, Oak Ridge, Tennessee.

price, it is not difficult to link energy demand to its price. Energy prices in real terms declined from as early as 1951 to 1973 and then sharply increased. Thus energy demand and price reveal a high correlation. One may conclude that low energy prices in the 1950s and 1960s stimulated demand growth and high prices in the 1970s did just the opposite. However, such a relationship between demand and price is by no means trivial, and furthermore, the extent to which demand responds to price cannot be easily determined by examining only the historical trends of demand and price. During the 1950s and 1960s real personal income and GNP increased rapidly and thus low energy prices could not be the sole promoter of energy demand. The decline in energy demand during 1974-75 was often attributed more to the economic recession which caused a decline in real personal income and GNP than to the sharp increases in energy price. Thus, it is essential to measure quantitatively the relative importance of various factors affecting energy demand. From a policy standpoint, understanding the effects of price on demand is particularly important because energy prices to some extent can be affected by policy actions. The purpose of this chapter is to provide statistical evidence of the demand-price relationship for several important energy sources used in various consuming sectors.

TABLE 2.1

Consumption of End-Use and Primary Energy
in the United States

| Consumption | 1961 | 1973 | 1976 | Percent Annual Growth Rate | |
	(quadrillion [10^{15}] Btu)			1961-73	1973-76
End-use energy	39	62	59	3.9	-1.7
Primary energy	46	76	73	4.3	-1.4

Source: U.S. Bureau of Mines.

Table 2.2 shows end-use energy consumption by fuel type and by consuming sector in the United States in 1976. In the residential and commercial sector, natural gas, petroleum products, and electricity are major end-use energy sources. Coal is another important

source of energy used in the industrial sector. The transportation
sector used predominately only petroleum products (97 percent).
In this chapter, we conduct two studies of energy demand at the
national level. One deals with demand for major fuels in the residential and commercial sector. The other deals with industrial demand for electricity.

TABLE 2.2

End-Use Energy Consumption in the United States
by Consuming Sector, 1976
(in trillion [10^{12}] Btu and percent)

Sector	Coal	Natural Gas	Petroleum	Electricity	Total
Residential and commercial	239	8,117	6,333	4,143	18,832
	(1)	(43)	(34)	(22)	(100)
Industrial	3,818	8,382	6,166	2,810	21,209[a]
	(18)	(40)	(29)	(13)	(100)
Transportation	0	582	18,733	16	19,331
	(0)	(3)	(97)	(0)	(100)
Total	4,057	17,081	31,232	6,969[b]	59,372
	(7)	(29)	(52)	(12)	(100)

[a]Includes 33 x 10^{12} Btu of hydropower.
[b]Generated from 21,367 x 10^{12} Btu of primary energy sources
(45 percent of coal, 15 percent of natural gas, 16 percent of petroleum products, 14 percent of hydropower, and 10 percent of nuclear
power).

Source: U.S. Bureau of Mines, Department of the Interior,
News release, March 14, 1977.

ENERGY DEMAND IN THE RESIDENTIAL
AND COMMERCIAL SECTOR

To evaluate the ultimate impacts of various energy pricing
policies, we need an integrated model that treats demands for all
substitute fuels interdependently. The purpose of this study is to
construct such an integrated energy demand model for the

residential/commercial sector. Specifically, a market-shares
model is developed in which demand elasticities for aggregate as
well as individual fuels are analytically derived.

In 1972 the household and commercial sectors used 18 quadrillion Btu of energy in the United States (Table 2.3). The largest
proportion of the energy was provided by natural gas, which accounted for 42 percent of the total. On the other hand, the use of
coal was almost negligible. Since utilization efficiencies vary remarkably among fuels, it is important to take into account these
differences when comparing the relative shares of individual fuels.
For space heating, Hise and Holman show that existing gas furnace
systems have utilization efficiencies of 50 to 60 percent, depending
upon the type of furnace and installation.[1] Oil furnace systems are
slightly less efficient than gas furnace systems. Utilization efficiency of coal for home heating is much less than that of oil and
natural gas.

TABLE 2.3

Quantities and Shares of End-Use Consumption of Fuels in the
U.S. Residential/Commercial Sector, 1972

Fuel	Before Adjustment[a]		After Adjustment[b]	
	Quantity (quadrillion Btu)	Share (percent)	Quantity (quadrillion Btu)	Share (percent)
Electricity	3.48	19	3.67	32
Natural gas	7.61	42	4.19	37
Petroleum products	6.67	37	3.34	30
Coal	0.31	2	0.11	1
Total	18.07	100	11.31	100

[a]These quantities are end-use figures. Therefore, the quantity
of electricity does not include power-plant losses, and the quantities
of natural gas, petroleum products, and coal do not include energy
used for drilling, mining, and distribution.

[b]Assumes a conversion efficiency factor of 1.0 for electricity,
0.55 for natural gas, 0.5 for petroleum products, and 0.35 for coal.

Source: U.S. Bureau of Mines, Fuel and Energy Data, United
States by States and Regions, 1972, information circular no. 8647
(Washington, D.C., 1974).

Most of the past studies concerning end-use efficiency have dealt with space heating. Since the bulk of natural gas and petroleum products was used for space heating, the relative end-use efficiencies of space heating are used as proxies for converting the aggregate energy use in the residential/commercial sector into an end-use basis. Because of the potential bias in applying these approximate efficiency factors, a sensitivity analysis for evaluating this bias was conducted and is discussed in the section entitled "Regression Results and Demand Elasticities." Based on the published sources[2] and on consultations with engineers, we selected efficiency factors of 1.0 for electricity, 0.55 for natural gas, 0.5 for oil, and 0.35 for coal as our base case. In applying these factors, original fuel consumption figures of Table 2.3 were adjusted to an end-use basis and are also shown in the same table. These adjustments increase the share of electricity significantly, even though natural gas still constitutes the largest share. Since changes in fuel mix may result in shifting from inefficient to more efficient fuels, in addition to changes in relative fuel prices, it is important to account for these relative efficiencies in interfuel substitution.

Historically, electricity prices have been higher than those for natural gas, oil, and coal. In 1972 the average price of electricity was $6.63 per million Btu, while prices of natural gas and No. 2 oil were $1.10 and $1.21, respectively (Table 2.4). After adjusting for relative utilization efficiencies, electricity still costs more than natural gas and oil (Table 2.4). These relative prices are important for explaining the behavior of households and commercial firms in their fuel choices.

The Market Shares Approach

One common approach to modeling energy demand is estimating a conventional demand function for a particular form of energy and investigating interfuel substitutions by including the prices of substitute fuels in the model. But this approach does not explicitly take into consideration interrelationships between consumption of a particular fuel and consumption of other fuels. The market-share approach developed here treats consumption of all substitutable fuels interdependently. The model consists of two parts: the first determines aggregate demand for energy in all forms, and the second estimates market shares for three major fuels (electricity, natural gas, and petroleum products). *

---

*Initially, we also included coal in the model. As it turned out, the price of coal was never significant in the share equations

TABLE 2.4

Average Prices of Fuels Used in the U.S.
Residential/Commercial Sector, 1972

Fuel	Average Price before Adjustment[a] (dollars/million Btu)	Average Price after Adjustment[b] (dollars/million Btu)
Electricity	6.63	6.63
Natural gas	1.10	2.00
No. 2 oil	1.21	2.42
Coal	0.32[c]	0.91
Weighted average	2.17[d]	3.55[e]

[a]Average prices in their common units are 22.6 mills per kwh (kilowatt hour) of electricity, $2.06 per MCF (thousand cubic feet) of natural gas, 17¢ per gallon of No. 2 oil, and $7.66 per ton of coal.

[b]Assumes a conversion efficiency factor of 1.0 for electricity, 0.55 for natural gas, 0.5 for oil, and 0.35 for coal.

[c]Based on f.o.b. (free on board) value.

[d]Computed using the shares of four fuels calculated from fuel-use quantities as the weighting factors.

[e]Computed using the shares of four fuels calculated from end-use quantities as weighting factors.

Source: Compiled by the author.

Aggregate energy demand is assumed to be a function of the weighted average energy price, personal income, and the numbers of heating and cooling degree days. The regression equation is expressed in linear form as follows:

$$Q = a_0 + a_1 P + a_2 I + a_3 H + a_4 C + a_5 D, \qquad (2.1)$$

of the other three fuels, and the prices of other fuels were not significant in the share equation for coal. Since the consumption of coal is of minimal magnitude in the residential and commercial sectors, we excluded this component from our analysis.

where $P = \sum_{i=1}^{3} P_i S_i$

$S_i = \dfrac{Q_i}{Q}$

a_i's are parameters to be estimated.

The market share for the ith fuel is assumed to be a function of its price, prices of substitute fuels, personal income, and degree days. The three market share equations have the following general form:

$$S_i = a_{10} + a_{i1}P_1 + a_{i2}P_2 + a_{i3}P_3 + a_{i4}I + a_{i5}H + a_{i6}C$$
$$+ a_{i7}D \qquad\qquad (2.2)$$

for i = 1, 2, 3

where a_{ij}'s are parameters to be estimated.
All variables are defined below:

Q_1 = Quantity of electricity demanded per capita in the residential and commercial sectors (thousands of Btu)

Q_2 = Quantity of natural gas demand per capita in the residential and commercial sectors (thousands of Btu)

Q_3 = Quantity of petroleum products demand per capita in the residential and commercial sectors (thousands of Btu)

Q = $Q_1 + Q_2 + Q_3$ = total quantity of energy demand per capita (trillions of Btu)

P_1 = Real average price of electricity used in the residential and commercial sectors (dollars per million Btu)

P_2 = Real average price of natural gas used in the residential and commercial sectors (dollars per million Btu)

P_3 = Real retail price of No. 2 fuel oil (dollars per million Btu)

I = Real per capita income (dollars)

H = Annual heating degree days weighted by population

C = Annual average cooling degree days

D = Dummy variable having value of 1 for 1971 and 0 for 1972.

All quantity variables (Q_i) and price variables (P_i) were adjusted according to the approximate relative end-use efficiencies of the three fuels as follows:

$$Q_i = \eta_i q_i \text{ and} \tag{2.3}$$

$$P_i = P_i / \eta_i$$

where q_i and p_i are, respectively, reported quantities and market prices, and η_i are the efficiency factors (1.0 for electricity, 0.55 for natural gas, and 0.5 for petroleum products).

The linear form is used because of the inclusion of degree days as variables. From engineering calculations, net heat loss from buildings is approximately proportional to the difference in temperature between the inside and the outside. Both theoretical considerations and direct observation indicate that fuel consumption for heating and cooling varies linearly with degree days when other factors are held constant.[3] Therefore, the use of the linear specification which preserves this important engineering relationship is necessary.

Recently, Nissen and Knapp[4] and Baughman and Joskow[5] have also estimated a two-component model similar to the one developed in this study. Baughman and Joskow estimated a set of multinomial logit functions. Their model specification imposes a very restrictive assumption (that is, all cross-price elasticities with respect to a given price are restricted to be identical).[6] Although Nissen and Knapp also estimated fuel-split (share) equations, our model differs from theirs in many respects. First, we use quantity shares rather than revenue shares as weighting factors for computing the weighted average price of energy. Our formulation, thus, provides a direct linkage between aggregate demand and market shares. More important, it facilitates the analytical derivation of demand elasticities. Second, income and degree-day variables appear in both aggregate-demand and share equations in our formulation. In the Nissen-Knapp model, no climatic variable was introduced, and income appeared only in the aggregate-demand equations. Finally, we adopt a linear specification; they used a log-linear specification. Under a linear specification, the fact that the market shares must sum up to 1 implies that

$$\sum_{i=1}^{3} a_{i0} = 1 \text{ and} \tag{2.4}$$

$$\sum_{i=1}^{3} a_{ij} = 0 \text{ for } j = 1, \ldots, 7 \tag{2.5}$$

The sum of all constant terms in the market-share equations must equal unity, and the sum of the estimated coefficients for each variable must equal zero. These important properties cannot be easily imposed in the log-linear model used by Nissen and Knapp.

The Data

To estimate the model as specified in the previous section, complete data on the consumption of all energy sources must be available. Data on oil consumption by sector are particularly lacking. Fortunately the U.S. Bureau of Mines recently compiled detailed data on consumption of oil and other fuels on a state basis. Although the residential and commercial sectors have to be combined, we believe this set of data is the best available.

Specifically, annual data for 48 states (excludes Hawaii and Alaska) for 1971 and 1972 were used for this study. Data on total energy consumption of electricity, natural gas, and petroleum products were obtained from the U.S. Bureau of Mines (Fuel and Energy Data, United States by States and Regions, 1972, Bureau of Mines Information Circular 8647, 1974; and United States Energy Fact Sheets, 2972, February 1973). Average electricity prices were computed by dividing revenues by sales of electricity, by state, published by Edison Electric Institute (Statistical Yearbook of the Electric Utility Industry, for 1971 and 1972). Similarly, average natural gas prices were computed from the revenues and sales data published by American Gas Association (Gas Facts, 1971 and 1972). Data on No. 2 oil prices were obtained from Platt's Oil Price Handbook and Oilmanac for 1971 and 1972 (New York: McGraw-Hill). Market spot (or terminal) price is available for only 56 major cities. For those states without any reported city, data for an adjacent state were used. We adjusted these terminal prices to retail prices by assuming a fixed percent of markup (65 percent).

State data on heating degree days (average weighted population over divisions) were obtained from the National Climatic Center, Asheville, N.C. ("Monthly Heating Degree Days by State and Season," Job No. 14624, November 13, 1973). Data on cooling degree days by city were obtained from National Oceanic and Atmospheric Administration (Climatological Data, National Summary, December 1971 and December 1972). City data were averaged to yield data for states.

Data on personal income were obtained from the Survey of Current Business, April 1974 (U.S. Department of Commerce). Population data were taken from Current Population Reports (U.S. Bureau of the Census).

Finally, all prices and income variables were deflated by the cost-of-living index. The 1970 state indexes derived by Anderson[7] were adjusted by the national consumer price index to obtain appropriate deflators for 1971 and 1972.

Regression Results and Demand Elasticities

The system of equations shown in equation 2.2 fits the general specification used by Zellner[8] for seemingly unrelated regressions. A proper procedure to estimate this set of share equations subject to constraints expressed in equations 2.4 and 2.5 is Zellner's generalized least-squares approach. One difficulty arises: Since all shares sum to unity, the disturbances across the three share equations will always add up to zero for each observation. As a result, the variance-covariance matrix is singular and nondiagonal. Berndt and Wood encountered the same problem in their study of industrial demand for energy in which translog cost functions were used.[9] They arbitrarily dropped one equation and estimated the remaining equations with linear restrictions with the iterative three-stage least-squares procedure. Unfortunately, this method could not be applied here because the constraints implied in our model are no longer needed when one share equation is dropped. Thus, if only two out of three share equations are estimated, Zellner's estimation procedure reduces to ordinary least squares (OLS), since we have the same set of independent variables. Hence, the present model is a special case of Zellner's model that conforms to the classical multivariate regression model.[10] In this case, OLS gives efficient estimators because the covariance matrix factors out of the Kronecker product relationships (disregarding constraints). Furthermore, since the constraints are automatically satisfied by OLS (as shown by Pindyck and Rubinfeld[11]), the OLS estimators must be efficient whether constraints are imposed in the multivariate regression or not. It is concluded, therefore, that OLS is the best method for estimating equation 2.2 alone.

The regression results are presented in Table 2.5. The overall performance of the model is remarkably good in terms of signs and statistical significance of the estimated coefficients. R^2s are reasonably high because this is essentially a cross-section analysis. *

---

*Although we used data for two years, the model is expected to explain primarily cross-sectional differences. Indeed, this was

TABLE 2.5

Estimated Aggregate Demand and Market-Share Equations

Type of Fuel	Dependent Variable	Energy Price (P)	Electricity Price (P_1)	Gas Price (P_2)	Oil Price (P_3)	Income (I)	Heating Degree Days (H)	Cooling Degree Days (C)	Yearly Dummy (D)	Constant	R^{2a}	Degrees of Freedom
Aggregate demand	Q	-10785[b] (1984)				5.521[b] (1.82)	3.331[b] (0.72)	3.627 (2.28)	-1473 (1514)	48060[b] (11400)	0.609	90
Electricity share	Q_1/Q x 1,000		-70.95[b] (6.29)	32.01[b] (6.62)	68.75[c] (30.6)	0.034[b] (0.012)	0.0036 (0.006)	0.107[b] (0.02)	-21.95[c] (10.3)	255.3[d] (143)	0.851	88
Natural gas share	Q_2/Q x 1,000		55.32[b] (9.28)	-190.41[b] (9.78)	103.97[c] (45.2)	0.026 (0.02)	-0.0131 (0.009)	-0.065[c] (0.02)	-2.79 (15.2)	178.8 (211)	0.816	88
Share of petroleum products	Q_3/Q x 1,000		15.63[d] (8.12)	158.40[c] (8.55)	-172.72[b] (39.5)	-0.060[b] (0.016)	0.0095 (0.008)	-0.042[d] (0.02)	24.74[d] (13.2)	565.9[b] (184)	0.876	88

Note: Figures in parentheses are estimated standard errors.

[a] R^2 is the multiple coefficient of determination.
[b] Statistically significant at the 1 percent level.
[c] Statistically significant at the 5 percent level.
[d] Statistically significant at the 10 percent level.

Source: Calculated by the author.

TABLE 2.6

Comparison of Aggregate Demand Elasticities

Model	Energy Price (P)	Income (I)
Present study	-0.70	0.41
Nissen-Knapp	-0.53	0.48
Baughman-Joskow	-0.80	0.62

Source: Compiled by the author.

Results for aggregate demand in Table 2.5 show that energy price and income coefficients are statistically significant. Furthermore, the coefficients of degree days all have the expected positive sign, and the heating-degree-day variable is more significant than the cooling-degree-day variable.

The coefficient estimates in the market-share equations are all plausible. All own-price and cross-price coefficients have the expected signs and are statistically significant. With respect to income effects, results show that an increase in income would increase market shares for electricity and natural gas and reduce the share for petroleum products. For heating degree days, the results suggest that the share of petroleum products in colder states is higher than the shares of natural gas and electricity. On the other hand, the results show that higher cooling degree days increase the share of electricity while reducing the shares of natural gas and petroleum products. These results are, of course, obvious because electricity is the major fuel used for air conditioning. The estimated coefficients for the dummy variable indicate that relatively more electricity was used in 1972 than in 1971. This increase may reflect a switch toward electricity because of the uncertainty about the assured availability of oil and natural gas.

By using the sample mean values, the aggregate-demand elasticities were computed to be -0.70 with respect to price and 0.41 with respect to income. Since the model is estimated from cross-sectional data, the resulting elasticities are generally interpreted

---

found to be the case. As we estimated the same model (without D) for 1971 and 1972 separately, the resulting estimates were very similar.

as long-run elasticities.[12] The present estimate of price elasticity falls between the estimates obtained by Nissen-Knapp[13] and Baughman-Joskow[14] (Table 2.6). Our estimate of income elasticity is lower than both of theirs.

Since the estimated income elasticity is well below unity, raising incomes would not result in a proportional rise in energy demand. A greater proportion of additional income would be spent for other consumer goods and services if prices of energy remain constant. The estimated price elasticity is also below unity, implying that an increase could be expected in consumer expenditures on energy as the price of energy rises.

Based on individual market-share equations, we can compute the market-share elasticities. The price elasticities have the following general expression:

$$e_{ij} = \frac{\partial S_i}{\partial P_j} \frac{\bar{P}_j}{\bar{S}_i} = a_{ij} \frac{\bar{P}_j}{\bar{S}_i} \text{ for } i, j = 1, 2, 3 \qquad (2.6)$$

where the "bar" indicates the mean values of sample data. It can be shown that these market-share elasticities are equivalent to the conditional demand elasticities. That is,

$$\eta_{ij} = \frac{\partial Q_i}{\partial P_j} \frac{\bar{P}_j}{\bar{Q}_i} \Bigg|_{\bar{Q}} = a_{ij} \frac{\bar{P}_j}{\bar{Q}_i} \bar{Q} = a_{ij} \frac{\bar{P}_j}{\bar{S}_i}$$

where aggregate demand Q remains unchanged.

The matrix of computed conditional-demand elasticities is presented in Table 2.7. This elasticity matrix may be intrepreted column by column. For example, elasticities in the first column show that an increase in electricity price by 1.0 percent would reduce long-run electricity demand by 1.34 percent and increase demands for natural gas and petroleum products by 1.0 and 0.3 percent, respectively, holding aggregate energy demand unchanged. As noted in the matrix, the substitutability between natural gas and petroleum products appears to be greater than either between electricity and natural gas or between electricity and petroleum products. The estimated elasticity matrix is not symmetric. This lack of symmetry can be explained by the fact that different fuels may be used for different purposes. For some end-use functions, substitution is simply not feasible or practical. For example, electricity used for lighting and air conditioning is generally considered non-substitutable, even though candles and gas air conditioners do exist.

TABLE 2.7

Estimated Conditional Demand Elasticities
Given Aggregate Demand
(computed at sample means)

Type of Fuel	Electricity Price (P_1)	Gas Price (P_2)	Oil Price (P_3)	Income (I)
Electricity	-1.341	0.250	0.547	0.403
Natural gas	9.990	-1.259	0.788	0.297
Petroleum products	0.275	1.090	-1.378	-0.715

Source: Calculated by the author from Table 2.5.

From the standpoint of conserving end-use energy, it is of great interest to know the aggregate-demand elasticities with respect to individual fuel prices. These elasticities can be computed from our model. Differentiating equation 2.1 with respect to the price of fuel j and using equation 2.2, we can derive:

$$\frac{\partial Q}{\partial P_j} = a_1 \left(S_j + \sum_{i=1}^{3} P_i a_{ij} \right) \text{ for } i = 1, 2, 3 \qquad (2.7)$$

The elasticity can then be computed by

$$e_j = \frac{\partial Q}{\partial P_j} \frac{\overline{P}_j}{\overline{Q}} = a_1 \left(\overline{S}_j + \sum_{i=1}^{3} \overline{P}_i a_{ij} \right) \frac{\overline{P}_j}{\overline{Q}} \qquad (2.8)$$

These elasticities are computed to be -0.054 for electricity price, -0.264 for natural gas price, and -0.270 for oil price. The fact that these elasticities are all negative has an important implication for energy conservation. It suggests that pricing strategies can be effective instruments for achieving energy conservation. These elasticities are partial elasticities in the sense that their interpretation requires an assumption of holding all other factors constant. If the prices of other fuels increase simultaneously, as is generally the case, the resulting energy conservation would be greater than implied by these elasticities.

Another notable feature of our market-share approach is that the conventional demand elasticities are derivable analytically. To derive the own-price elasticity, we differentiate question 2.2 with respect to P_j:

$$\frac{\partial S_j}{\partial P_j} = \frac{1}{Q} \frac{\partial Q_j}{\partial P_j} - \frac{Q_j}{Q^2} \frac{\partial Q}{\partial P_j} \tag{2.9}$$

Substituting equation 2.7 into equation 2.9 and equating the resulting equation to a_{ii}, we obtain

$$\frac{\partial Q_j}{\partial P_j} = a_{jj} Q + a_1 S_j \left(S_j + \sum_{i=1}^{3} P_i a_{ij} \right)$$

Hence, the conventional own-price elasticity can be computed by

$$E_{jj} = \frac{\partial Q_j}{\partial \bar{P}_j} \frac{\bar{P}_j}{\bar{Q}_j} = \left[a_{jj} \bar{Q} + a_1 \bar{S}_j \left(\bar{S}_j + \sum_{i=1}^{3} \bar{P}_i a_{ij} \right) \right] \frac{\bar{P}_j}{\bar{Q}_j} \tag{2.10}$$

Note that equation 2.10 can be alternatively expressed by

$$E_{jj} = \frac{\partial S_j}{\partial P_j} \frac{\bar{P}_j}{\bar{S}_j} + \frac{\partial Q}{\partial P_j} \frac{\bar{P}_i}{\bar{Q}} \tag{2.11}$$

if the equality holds as follows:

$$\bar{S}_j = \frac{\bar{Q}_j}{\bar{Q}} \tag{2.12}$$

Equation 2.11 states that the conventional-demand elasticity can be expressed as the sum of the market-share elasticity as previously determined in equation 2.6 and the aggregate-demand elasticity shown in equation 2.8. However, if we use the sample means for computation, the equality (2.12) does not hold in general. Hence, it is more appropriate to use equation 2.10 rather than equation 2.11, even though the differences are found to be very small.

Similarly, cross-price elasticity can be expressed as follows:

$$E_{jk} = \frac{\partial Q_j}{\partial P_k} \frac{\overline{P}_k}{\overline{Q}_j} = \left[a_{jk} \overline{Q} + a_1 \overline{S}_j \left(\overline{S}_k + \sum_{i=1}^{3} \overline{P}_i \, a_{ik} \right) \right] \frac{\overline{P}_k}{\overline{Q}_j} \qquad (2.13)$$

and income elasticity as

$$E_{ji} = \frac{\partial Q_j}{\partial I} \frac{\overline{I}}{\overline{Q}_j} = (a_{j4} \overline{Q} + a_2 \overline{S}_j) \frac{\overline{I}}{\overline{Q}_j}$$

The conventional-unconditional-demand elasticities computed at the mean values of sample data are presented in Table 2.8. The estimates of own-price elasticities are all greater than 1.0 and this indicates that demands for all fuels are price elastic. Although the negative elasticity of natural gas price for electricity demand is not expected, its magnitude is small. This result does not seem too surprising, because most electricity demand studies have obtained either insignificant or small cross-price elasticities with respect to natural gas.

TABLE 2.8

Estimated Conventional Demand Elasticities

Type of Fuel	Electricity Price (P_1)	Gas Price (P_2)	Oil Price (P_3)	Income (I)
Electricity	-1.461	-0.015	0.290	0.856
Natural gas	0.919	-1.495	0.508	0.698
Petroleum products	0.215	0.806	-1.608	-0.293

Source: Calculated by the author from Table 2.5.

Considering natural gas demand, the two cross-price elasticities are high, and their sum is almost equal to the own-price elasticity. These results imply that changes in prices of electricity and oil would have substantial impacts on natural gas demand. However, if all fuel prices changed by the same percentage, the impact on natural gas demand would be minimal because the own-price effect is offset by the cross-price effects. The same conclusion does not hold for electricity and petroleum products demands where the sum of cross-price elasticities is smaller than the own-price elasticity. In the demand for petroleum products, natural gas is a much more important substitute than electricity. Furthermore, estimated income elasticities are positive but smaller than unity for electricity and natural gas. A negative income elasticity for petroleum products is not expected although the magnitude is small.

The present estimates of own-price elasticities are slightly higher than those estimates obtained by Baughman and Joskow[15] and much higher than the estimates of Nissen and Knapp.[16] Also, our estimates of cross-price elasticities of the demands for natural gas and petroleum products are higher than those obtained by Baughman and Joscow. We note that they derived their demand elasticities using a simulation procedure, and one cannot be sure that the resulting estimates are independent of the particular assumptions they used in their simulations.

Our model was estimated assuming efficiency factors of 1.0 for electricity, 0.55 for natural gas, and 0.5 for petroleum products. Although these assumptions are the best to our knowledge, they are by no means absolutely accurate. It is therefore important to know how sensitive the resulting elasticity estimates are to these assumptions. To assess this sensitivity, we reran the regressions for four other alternative sets of efficiency assumptions. A detailed comparison of the resulting estimates of conventional demand elasticities for individual fuels is presented in Table 2.9. The results show that the elasticity estimates are not sensitive to the assumptions made on end-use efficiencies within the range of uncertainty.

Demand and Conservation of Primary Energy

The analyses presented in the previous two sections dealt with energy used by households and commercial firms for performing various end-use functions. The elasticities obtained from these analyses measure the extent to which consumers respond to changes in economic and climatic factors in determining the amount of energy they actually use. However, these elasticities do not measure directly the response of demand to these exogenous changes for primary energy sources. By primary energy, we mean the energy sources used to produce fuels for end use.* For example, coal,

----

*We broaden our definition of primary energy here to include energy required to produce other energy sources besides electricity at points of end uses.

TABLE 2.9

Comparison of the Conventional Demand Elasticities for Alternative
Assumptions on Efficiency Factors

Assumed Efficiency Conversion Factor, η		Type of Fuel	Electricity Price	Gas Price	Oil Price	Income
Natural Gas	Oil					
0.4	0.4	Electricity	-1.385	-0.045	0.237	0.731
		Natural gas	0.918	-1.509	0.597	0.704
		Petroleum products	0.219	0.801	-1.617	-0.325
0.5	0.5	Electricity	-1.444	-0.027	0.280	0.824
		Natural gas	0.931	1.502	0.557	0.693
		Petroleum products	0.194	0.781	-1.615	-0.276
0.6	0.6	Electricity	-1.486	-0.011	0.320	0.910
		Natural gas	0.946	-1.498	0.523	0.691
		Petroleum products	0.179	0.768	-1.615	-0.236
0.8	0.8	Electricity	-1.559	0.020	0.297	1.057
		Natural gas	0.959	-1.489	0.473	0.694
		Petroleum products	0.150	0.755	-1.612	-0.169

Source: Compiled by the author.

natural gas, oil, hydropower, and uranium are used to generate
electricity; electricity, natural gas, and oil are required fuels for
drilling natural gas and oil.

To properly evaluate the potential for energy conservation,
we need to examine the primary energy sources needed to meet the
final demands for end-use fuels.

To analyze the primary energy demand in our model, we must
first convert our end-use energy to primary energy, assuming fixed
input-output relationships, and then compute the price elasticities
for primary energy demand. From equation 2.3, we have

$$q_i = \frac{Q_i}{\eta_i}$$

where q_i = reported quantity of fuel i without adjustment for end-
use efficiency

η = end-use efficiency factor of fuel i

Q_i = adjusted quantity of fuel i used in our previous estimation.

Note that q_i and Q_i were expressed on a per-capita basis. Let M_i be
the amount of primary energy used to produce q_i. Furthermore, M_i
can be expressed as:

$$M_i = \epsilon_i q_i$$

where ϵ_i is the input-output coefficient measuring the amount of primary energy required to produce a unit of fuel i for end-uses.
Hence, the total primary energy demand can be expressed as

$$M = \sum_{i=1}^{3} M_i = \sum_{i=1}^{3} \frac{\epsilon_i}{\eta_i} Q_i \qquad (2.14)$$

In our formulation, the overall efficiency in using primary energy
in homes and commercial buildings can be defined as

$$\delta_i = \frac{\eta_i}{\epsilon_i} \qquad (2.15)$$

Equation 2.14 can then be rewritten as:

$$M = \sum_{i=1}^{3} \frac{Q_i}{\epsilon_i} \qquad (2.16)$$

It must be noted that we are interested only in the total primary energy, disregarding the mixture of primary energy sources used for generating electricity or drilling natural gas. Herendeen and Bullard have shown that the overall input-output coefficients for converting primary energy to electricity, natural gas, and petroleum products changed only slightly between 1963 and 1967.[17]

To examine the impacts of changes in fuel prices on primary energy demand, we differentiate equation 2.16 with respect to the individual fuel prices:

$$\frac{\partial M}{\partial P_j} = \sum_{i=1}^{3} \frac{1}{\delta_i} \frac{\partial Q_i}{\partial P_j}$$

The price elasticities of the demand for primary energy can then be computed by

$$\lambda_j = \frac{\partial M}{\partial P_j} \frac{\bar{P}_j}{\bar{M}} = \left[\sum_{i=1}^{3} (\frac{1}{\delta_i}) \frac{\partial Q_i}{\partial P_j} \right] \frac{\bar{P}_j}{\bar{M}} \quad \text{for } j = 1,\, 2,\, 3 \quad (2.17)$$

For computing these elasticities, we note that the partial derivatives, $\partial Q_i / \partial P_j$, have been previously evaluated in equations 2.9 and 2.10 using sample means. The total efficiency factors (δ_i) are computed based on the 1967 input-output coefficients estimated by Herendeen and Bullard.[18] These estimates are shown in Table 2.10. Accounting for the direct and indirect usage of energy in producing end-use fuels, electricity becomes the least efficient fuel with an overall efficiency of 26 percent. The last figure needed for computing price elasticities is the mean value of M, which is obtained from equation 2.16 using the mean values of Q_i.

In Table 2.11 the resulting estimates of price elasticities using equation 2.17 are compared with the estimates previously obtained using equation 2.8 for total end-use energy. A striking difference was found in the estimated elasticity of electricity price. The magnitude of the electricity price elasticity (-0.33) for primary energy demand is much higher than that of the prices of natural gas and oil, while it is the lowest (-0.05) among the three price elasticities for end-use energy demand. This is clearly due to the fact that the total efficiency for using electricity is much lower than that of natural gas and petroleum products. The results show that raising electricity prices would be more effective in conserving primary energy than raising prices of natural gas and oil. This is, of course, in sharp contrast to the conclusion reached for end-use energy demand, which showed the opposite. These results are not contradictory; rather, they show that it is essential to distinguish between end-use energy and primary energy for making policy decisions concerning energy conservation.

TABLE 2.10

Total Efficiency Factors by Fuel Type

Type of Fuel	End-use Efficiency (η_i)	Input-Output Coefficient for Converting Primary Energy (ϵ_i)	Total Efficiency Factor $(\delta_i=\eta_i/\lambda_i)$
Electricity	1.00	3.796	0.263
Natural gas	0.55	1.101	0.500
Petroleum products	0.50	1.208	0.414

Source: Compiled by the author.

TABLE 2.11

Comparison of Estimated Price Elasticities for Total End-Use Energy and Primary Energy

Type of Demand	Electricity Price (P_1)	Gas Price (P_2)	Oil Price (P_3)
End-use energy	-0.054	-0.264	-0.270
Primary energy	-0.330	-0.157	-0.224

Source: Compiled by the author.

Conclusions

This study shows that aggregate end-use energy demand in the residential/commercial sector has a price elasticity of -0.7, while individual fuel demands are all price elastic in the long run. Furthermore, changes in the price of a particular fuel would affect its demand more than the aggregate energy demand because of interfuel substitution. For example, an increase of 1 percent in electricity price would reduce electricity demand by 1.4 percent and reduce total end-use energy demand by 0.1 percent. With a 1 percent increase in price of natural gas, the resulting demand reductions for natural gas and for total end-use energy would be 1.5 and 0.2 percent, respectively. A 1 percent increase in the price of oil would reduce demand by 1.6 percent and the aggregate end-use energy demand by 0.3 percent. Hence, raising petroleum prices appears to have the strongest potential for conserving end-use energy.

When primary energy is considered, the results show that the elasticity of electricity price is higher than that of prices of natural gas and oil. This higher elasticity indicates that increasing the price of electricity has a greater impact on reducing demand for primary energy. The study concludes that it is essential to distinguish primary energy from end-use energy for making policy decisions.

The model constructed in this chapter explains the consumer's response to changes in various explanatory variables. Since cross-sectional data were used for the estimations, the results characterize interstate variation as well as behavioral relationships. There are potential causes that may induce changes in the demand structure in the future. For example, new technologies such as solar heating and the Annual Cycle Energy System (ACES) may be widely adopted. Also, there may be significant changes in life styles so that people prefer smaller and multiunit housing. Therefore, the energy conservation resulting from higher prices may be greater than our historical elasticities indicate. The fact that consumers do respond to price changes, as shown in this and other studies, suggests that significant potential exists for adopting energy-conserving technologies in this era of increasing energy prices.

The model has at least two limitations regarding its usefulness for forecasting. First, a model based on cross-sectional analysis provides only estimates of long-run demand elasticities. In forecasting, it is necessary to deal with both short- and long-run effects. Second, although our linear model assures that the estimated market shares always sum to unity, it does not guarantee that the estimated shares are all positive. Despite these limitations, the model gives a better analytical insight into the demand structure than other models that use log or logit form.

Furthermore, we used average prices of electricity and natural gas in this study. Due to a declining block pricing for electricity and natural gas, the use of average prices may result in a simultaneous equation bias as discussed. Thus our estimates of elasticities associated with prices of electricity and natural gas may be somewhat biased.

Finally, we should also point out that our model does not deal
with interrelationships between the price of electricity and the prices
of natural gas and oil. Since natural gas and petroleum products
have been among the major energy sources for generating electricity,
changes in prices of natural gas and oil will affect the price of electricity. Hence, any policy instruments, such as the deregulation of
the prices of natural gas and oil designed to affect prices of natural
gas and oil, will also affect the price of electricity. We anticipate,
however, that the significance of these relationships will diminish in
the future when the nation possibly moves toward using more abun-
dant energy sources such as coal and nuclear power for electric
generation.

INDUSTRIAL DEMAND FOR ELECTRICITY

Numerous econometric studies for electricity demand, though
mostly for the residential sector, are available in the literature.
These studies can be classified into three groups based on what
electricity price measure was used in the model. The first group
includes those using average price in a single equation model.
Major contributors in this group include Anderson,[19] Chern et al.,[20]
Fisher and Kaysen,[21] Griffin,[22] Mount et al.,[23] and Wilson.[24] The
second group of studies adopted marginal prices of some kind such
as Typical Electric Bills used by Houthakker et al.[25] and some
weighted averages of representative in actual rate schedules used by
Taylor et al.[26] The final group used average price in a simultaneous
equation system. Important studies in this category include those of
Halvorsen,[27] Wilder and Willenborg,[28] and Chern.[29]
Even though economists have paid increasing attention to the
estimation of electricity demand, the area of industrial demand remains relatively untouched. Most previous studies of industrial demand have used cross-section Census data at the standard industrial
classification (SIC) two-digit level. In an early study, Fisher and
Kaysen[30] estimated an electricity demand equation for ten two-digit
SIC manufacturing industries, using 1956 Census data for 47 states.
They expressed the total electricity purchased and generated by the
i[th] industry as a function of the value added and the average cost per
kilowatt hour of purchased electricity for this industry. Wilson[31]
later applied the Fisher-Kaysen model to 15 SIC two-digit industries
and used the 1963 Census data for Standard Metropolitan Statistical
Area (SMSA) cities. These models obviously are unsuitable for estimating the long-run adjustment behavior over time. Furthermore,
both studies failed to examine the possible interfuel substitution

between electricity and other energy sources. * Despite their short-
comings, all of these studies generally support the conclusion that
the industrial demand for electricity is highly responsive to changes
in its own price.[†]

This study represents an extension of the author's earlier
study of industrial demand for electricity using a simultaneous equation model. The earlier analysis is extended to cover the entire
manufacturing sector, and furthermore the specification of the
model is also improved. Specifically, a dynamic electricity demand model for major SIC three-digit manufacturing industries is
developed and estimated. The study focuses on the estimation of
price response, interfuel substitution, and the impact of technological change.

The Problem of Simultaneity

To illustrate the problem of simultaneity involved in this
study, let us consider a traditional market model:

$$\text{Demand } q = D\,(p,y) \tag{2.18}$$

$$\text{Supply } p = S\,(q,c) \tag{2.19}$$

It is known that inclusion of income (y) and cost (c) variables in the
demand and supply relations, respectively, typically yield an identi-
fiable set of estimating equations. If the supply curve is a function
of costs alone, that is, the supply curve is perfectly elastic, then
the model is recursive. A similar result holds if the demand curve
is invariant with respect to price. In the context of electricity demand, the appropriate representation for equation 2.18 is

$$q = D\,(r,y) \tag{2.20}$$

---

*In 1971 the total energy sources purchased by the manufac-
turing sector consisted of 32 percent of electricity, 40 percent of
natural gas, 10 percent of coal, 9 percent of fuel oil, and 9 percent
of all other energy sources.

[†]In contrast to this general finding, Baxter and Rees, using
British data, have found in their elaborated geometric lag model
that the electricity demand is highly responsive to changes in output
and fuel technology but relatively unresponsive to price. See R. F.
Baxter and R. Rees, "Analysis of Industrial Demand for Electricity,"
Economic Journal 78 (June 1968): 277-98.

where r represents the relevant block tariff schedule. The standard simultaneity problem associated with demand and supply analysis thereby hinges on the relation between the designated rate schedule and quantity purchased. If the rate schedule depends upon exogenous factors, the model will be recursive in nature. The problem, there-fore, lies in how to represent the rate schedule. When ex post prices, either average or marginal, are used, simultaneous equa-tions bias is introduced. Mathematically,

$$q = D (P_a, y) \qquad\qquad (2.21)$$

$$P_a = S (q, c) \qquad\qquad (2.22)$$

where P_a is an ex post proxy for the true rate schedule. Equation 2.22 is not a supply equation in the traditional sense; it is really a price equation facing electricity customers. We recognize, of course, that if we use an ex ante price from actual rate schedules, the problem of bias can be avoided. However, it would be an enor-mous task to construct the necessary data base on ex ante prices for our study. Furthermore, available evidence based on the re-cent results of Taylor et al. does not seem to justify such an effort. Using the marginal prices constructed from actual rate schedules, Taylor et al. estimated the own-price elasticity to be -0.8 for resi-dential demand.[32] They claimed that it is significantly lower than -1.0 obtained from several other studies using average price. We note that Griffin, using average price and a polynomial lag formula-tion, obtained an elasticity estimate as low as -0.5.[33] Thus, a higher elasticity obtained from other studies using average price cannot be easily attributed solely to a bias of using average price. Admittedly, more evidence is needed to resolve this controversy.

Equations 2.21 and 2.22 form the fundamental system used to characterize the interaction of demand and price. These demand and price equations need to be specified in more detail for the econo-metric analysis.

Electricity is generally used by industrial firms for environ-mental control, machine operation, and chemical processes. En-vironmental uses of electricity include lighting, cooling, and heat-ing of buildings. These uses are only indirectly related to indus-trial production and constitute a minor portion of electricity used by industry. The bulk of electricity is used for operating machin-ery and as inputs to various chemical processes. Thus electricity demand is derived from the demand for durable goods like appliances or machinery. Consequently, it is necessary to distinguish short-run versus long-run behaviors of electricity customers. In the short run, demand response is primarily a result of changing

utilization rates of existing stock of appliances and/or equipment.
In the long run, both utilization rate and stock of appliances can be
altered in response to changes in exogenous factors such as prices
of fuels.

We examined several dynamic demand formulations including
the flow-adjustment models of Houthakker-Taylor type[34] and of
linear semilogarithmic and logarithmic Koyck models and found
that the logarithmic Koyck model yielded the most plausible results.
Taylor et al. also found similar results for the residential sector.[35]

To illustrate how the price (supply) equation is formulated in
this study, we assume the average price of electricity for an industry can be approximated by

$$P_i = \beta_i Q_i^{\beta_1} C^{\beta_2} \tag{2.23}$$

where P_i = average price paid by industry i

Q_i = quantity purchased by industry i

C = cost per kwh.

The parameters $\beta_0, \beta_1, \beta_2$, are to be estimated. Taking logarithmic transformation, equation 2.23 becomes

$$\ln P_i = \ln \beta_o + \beta_1 \ln Q_i + \beta_2 \ln C \tag{2.24}$$

we expect β_1 to be negative and β_2 to be positive. In the econometric model the cost variable is split into several components.

Econometric Specification

Since the logarithmic Koyck model is used to characterize the
dynamic demand structure, the long-run electricity demand for a
manufacturing industry (say the ith industry) is specified as:

$$\ln E_{it} = \alpha_o + \alpha_1 \ln E_{i,t-1} + \alpha_2 \ln EP_{it} + \alpha_3 \ln X_{it} + U_{it} \tag{2.25}$$

where t stands for time period

    E   is the amount of electricity purchased and generated
          (millions of kwh)

    EP is the real average price of electricity in cents per kwh,
          deflated by the wholesale price index (WPI) of intermediate
          materials, supplies, and components (1967 = 100)

    χ   refers to a set of explanatory variables

    U   represents the disturbance term

    αs   are parameters to be estimated.

The set of explanatory variables (X) includes the following:

    GP = real average natural gas price (dollars per thousand therms)

    PP = wholesale price index of refined petroleum products (1967 = 100) deflated by WPI

    CP = wholesale price index of coal (1967 = 100) deflated by WPI

    W   = average wage rate for manufacturing production workers (dollars per hour) deflated by WPI

    V   = value added (millions of dollars)

    T   = time trend variable (1958 = 1, 1959 = 2, and so on).

The rationale for including those explanatory variables should be clear in most cases. The prices of coal, natural gas, and petroleum products are used to measure the extent to which interfuel substitution had occurred. The estimated parameters of these variables are termed cross-price elasticities and they are expected to have a positive sign. The time-trend variable is included to measure the impact of technological change which is expected to occur over time. The sign of this variable cannot be a priori determined.

The price equation has the following general form:

$$\ln EP_{it} = \beta_0 + \beta_1 \ln E_{it} + \beta_2 Z_t + V_{it} \tag{2.26}$$

where Z refers to a set of explanatory variables

    V represents the disturbance term

    βs are parameters to be estimated

    EP and E are defined previously.

The set of variables (Z) includes:

    FC   = cost of fuels used for generation (cents per kwh)

    OMC = total operating expense net of fuel and purchased power payment (cents per kwh)

    CC   = capital input costs (cents per kwh)

    RE   = the ratio of industrial sales to total sales of electricity (percent).

Variables FC, OMC, and CC cover all essential cost components of electric generation, transmission, and distribution. We expect these cost variables to have a positive coefficient. Since transmission and distribution costs per kilowatt hour sold are expected to be lower for industrial sales than for residential and commercial sales, the variable RE is included to account for the possible effects of the composition of the total sales on the price of electricity to industrial customers. In equation 2.26, average electricity price (EP) as the left-hand variable is not deflated by the wholesale price index. This specification of the price equation represents more appropriately the electric rate schedule than the alternative using deflated electricity price. The same treatment was also previously adopted by Halvorsen.

The Data

The quantity of electricity as the dependent variable in the demand equation includes both purchased and self-generated electricity. Average electricity price is obtained by dividing costs by quantity of the purchased electricity. Data on the quantity (E) and price (EP) of electricity and value added (V) were obtained from the U.S. Bureau of the Census (Census of Manufacturers; Annual Survey of Manufacturers, selected years). Data on costs of fuels used for generation (FC) and the ratio of industrial sales to total sales of electric utilities (RE) were taken from Edison Electric Institute's Statistical Yearbook of Electric Utility Industry, 1958-71. For natural gas price (PG), we used data published by the American Gas Association (Gas Facts and Historical Statistics of the Gas Industry). Data on operating and maintenance expenses (OMC) and capital input costs (CC) were compiled by the Federal Power Commission based on Statistics of Privately Owned Electric Utilities. For the price indexes of coal (CP), petroleum products (PP), and intermediate materials (WPI), data were published by the U.S. Department of Commerce (Survey of Current Business).

The variables E, EP, V, and W are observed at the SIC three-digit industry level. Data on GP are not available for all SIC three-digit industries. In some cases, data for the corresponding two-digit industry were used. Variables PP, CP, and WPI are aggregate price indexes for the entire industry sector. On the other hand, FC, OMC, CC, and RE are aggregate variables for the electric utility industry. All data were collected for the period of 1958-71.

Regression Results and Demand Elasticities

Fifteen SIC three-digit industries were selected for the analysis. The preliminary statistical testing of the model indicates that estimating this system of equations for each individual industry is

difficult because of the small sample size and high correlation between the lagged dependent variable and other explanatory variables
in equation 2.25. One way to overcome these difficulties is to increase the sample size by pooling industries together.

   Since demand structure is expected to vary somewhat among
different industries, it is desirable to group together only those with
a similar demand structure. Several pooling criteria were tried.
Among those criteria which proved ineffective were the degree of
electric-intensiveness and the magnitudes of the short-run price
elasticities previously estimated by Chern.[36] The only pooling criterion which produced plausible results was the existence of significant electricity-gas substitution. Specifically, three groupings were
adopted. Assuming that the basic demand structure is the same,
Group A includes all 15 industries. Based on the results of the
static model previously estimated, Group B consists of 10 industries
with a significant substitution between electricity and gas.[37] Group
C is the class of industries in which gas is not an important substitute. The specific industries in each group are identified in Table
2.12.

   It should be mentioned that SIC-281 (Industrial Chemical) does
not include the U.S. Energy Research and Development Administration's (ERDA) three uranium enrichment plants. It is noted that
these three plants accounted for 58 percent of the electricity consumption in SIC 281 in 1958. This share declined to 18 percent in
1971. Since the electricity consumption by ERDA's plants is more
a function of government policies than of economic variables, it was
considered desirable to separate this component from the rest of
SIC-281.

   The statistical problem for estimating the simultaneous equations model specified in the previous section is complicated by the
presence of the lagged dependent variable and the correlation of
residuals resulting from using pooled data. In the case of a single
equation, it is well known that the appropriate approaches are the
variance components models developed by Wallace and Hussian,[38]
Maddala,[39] and Nerlove.[40] All these approaches employ a two-step
technique to run generalized least squares. As suggested by Nerlove,
to handle a dynamic equation, the appropriate method is to apply the
least-squares with dummy variables approach (LSDV) in the first
step and then use the LSDV residuals to estimate variance components
for the generalized least-squares estimation in the second step. We
applied the variance components model to estimate equation 2.25 and
found out that the results are almost identical to those obtained by
LSDV (these results are available in Chern[41]). This would be the
case if the variance of the dummies is large relative to the error
variance. These evidences, therefore, suggest that the proper pro-

cedure to estimate our simultaneous equations system should be the two-stage least-squares with dummy variables approach (TSLS). Since we have a time-trend term in the model, we include only cross-section dummies.

TABLE 2.12

Identification of Industry Groups

Group	Criterion for Grouping	SIC Code	Industry
A	None	All 15	industries
B	Gas is a significant substitute	281	Industrial chemicals
		331	Blast furnace and basic steel products
		291	Petroleum refining
		371	Motor vehicles and equipment
		282	Plastic materials and synthetics
		263	Paperboard mills
		203	Canned, cured, and frozen foods
		204	Grain mill products
		322	Glass and glassware
		225	Knitting mills
C	Gas is not a significant substitute	333	Primary nonferrous metals
		262	Paper mills
		324	Cement, hydraulic
		332	Iron and steel foundries
		221	Weaving mills, cotton

Source: Compiled by the author.

To appraise the validity of our simultaneous equation approach, we compare the performance of TSLS with LSDV. The latter approach does not consider the impact of simultaneity in the system and, thus, the estimates do not account for the effects of declining block-rate pricing.

The simultaneous equations model as specified above was fitted to annual national data over the 1959-71 period. Estimated demand and price equations are presented in Tables 2.13 and 2.14, respectively. The log-linear form was used, thus the estimated coefficients are short-run elasticities. Note that some relevant but less-important exogenous variables were not included in these final equations because either their coefficients had the incorrect sign or their inclusion disturbed the coefficients of other more important variables resulting possibly from the problem of multicollinearity.

We are primarily interested in the demand equations. All LSDV and TSLS estimates of the demand equations are plausible, as all estimated coefficients have the correct sign and most are statistically significant, at least at the 10 percent level. R^2s are all fairly high. It is noted, however, the TSLS estimate of the own-price coefficient is substantially lower than that obtained by LSDV in all three cases. Taylor has shown that the use of average price, in general, leads to an upward bias in the estimate of the price elasticity.[42] The comparison of TSLS and LSDV estimates does confirm this theoretical expectation and the simultaneous equations model seems able to reduce such a bias. Note further that the TSLS estimates are consistent while the LSDV estimates are not in our simultaneous equations model. All these considerations lead us to conclude that TSLS is superior to LSDV.

Let us evaluate the criterion for grouping by the electricity-gas substitution. In Group B, gas price is significant while it is not in Group C. Furthermore, the coefficient estimate of natural gas price is substantially larger in Group B than that in Group A. The impact of gas price is significantly reduced when all industries are pooled together. The coefficient estimates of coal price show a similar pattern with a larger magnitude in Group B than in Group A. No substitute fuels turn out to be significant in Group C. Furthermore, the estimated coefficient for the lagged dependent variable is higher in Group B than in Group C. This implies that the adjustment is slower for the former group. The computed mean lag is 2.6 years in Group B as compared to 1.4 years in Group C.

The time variable has a negative coefficient, indicating that electricity consumption has been declining over time, holding other factors constant. Since the value added was not deflated, the time variable may pick up the effects of the value deflator as well as the impacts of technological changes. * Although these effects cannot be

---

*The proper value deflator is not available for SIC three-digit industries. We could have used the wholesale price index of final output as the value deflator. But this is considered to be inappropriate. It

TABLE 2.13
Estimated Demand Equations
(normalized variable: $\ln E_i$)

Industry Group	Estimation Method	$\ln E_{i,t-1}$	$\ln EP_i$	$\ln V_i$	$\ln GP_i$	$\ln CP$	T	Constant	R^2[a]	Degrees of Freedom	Mean[b] Lag
A	LSDV	0.653[c] (0.05)	-0.584[c] (0.06)	0.362[c] (0.05)	0.178[d] (0.07)	0.078[d] (0.03)	-0.013[c] (0.003)	-4.86[c] (0.54)	0.998	174	1.9
	TSLS	0.726[c] (0.07)	-0.246[e] (0.14)	0.372[c] (0.05)	0.142[e] (0.08)	0.076[d] (0.03)	-0.011[c] (0.003)	-2.42[d] (1.05)	0.998	174	2.7
B	LSDV	0.666[c] (0.06)	-0.535[c] (0.07)	0.406[c] (0.07)	0.341[c] (0.10)	0.106[d] (0.04)	-0.016[c] (0.005)	-4.88[e] (0.66)	0.999	114	2.0
	TSLS	0.719[c] (0.08)	-0.370[d] (0.15)	0.428[c] (0.07)	0.347[c] (0.10)	0.110[c] (0.04)	-0.017[c] (0.005)	-3.921[c] (1.03)	0.998	114	2.6
C	LSDV	0.578[c] (0.07)	-0.499[c] (0.12)	0.340[c] (0.06)			-0.006[d] (0.003)	-3.452[e] (1.11)	0.998	56	1.4
	TSLS	0.584[c] (0.07)	-0.304[e] (0.18)	0.358[c] (0.06)			-0.004 (0.003)	-1.806 (1.55)	0.998	56	1.4

Note: Figures in parentheses are estimated standard errors.

[a] R is the correlation coefficient between the observed and estimated values of the normalized variable. Both LSDV and TSLS estimates of dummy coefficients are not presented here.

[b] Computed from $\alpha_1/(1 - \alpha_1)$, where (α_1) is the estimated coefficient of $\ln E_{i,t-1}$.

[c] Statistically significant at the 1 percent level.

[d] Statistically significant at the 5 percent level.

[e] Statistically significant at the 10 percent level.

Source: Calculated by the author.

TABLE 2.14

Estimated Price Equations

(normalized variable = ln EP_i)

Industry Group	Estimation Method	ln E_i	ln FC	ln OMC	ln RE	Constant	R^2[a]	Degrees of Freedom
A	LSDV	-0.278[b] (0.03)	0.090[d] (0.07)	0.394[c] (0.15)	-0.605[b] (0.15)	-2.85[b] (0.26)	0.981	176
	TSLS	-0.219[b] (0.03)	0.093[d] (0.07)	0.408[c] (0.17)	-0.410[b] (0.16)	-3.22[b] (0.27)	0.980	176
B	LSDV	-0.370[b] (0.04)	0.071 (0.09)	0.396[c] (0.22)	-1.012[b] (0.21)	-2.45 (0.31)	0.964	116
	TSLS	-0.325[b] (0.04)	0.069 (0.09)	0.405[c] (0.22)	-0.842[b] (0.23)	-2.65[b] (0.33)	0.964	116
C	LSDV	-0.147[b] (0.04)	0.168[c] (0.09)	0.391[c] (0.22)	-0.162 (0.19)	-3.55 (0.35)	0.993	56
	TSLS	-0.111[b] (0.04)	0.176[c] (0.09)	0.401[c] (0.22)	-0.077 (0.19)	-3.79[b] (0.36)	0.993	56

Note: Figures in parentheses are estimated standard errors.

[a] R is the correlation coefficient between the observed and estimated values of the normalized variable.

Both LSDV and TSLS estimates of dummy coefficients are not reported here.

[b] Statistically significant at the 1 percent level.

[c] Statistically significant at the 5 percent level.

[d] Statistically significant at the 10 percent level.

separated in the model, the fact that the time variable is not significant in Group C suggests that the effects of the value deflator are unlikely to be of any appreciable magnitude. Thus, it seems appropriate to conclude that industrial production processes have become
more and more efficient in using electricity, perhaps as a result of
technological improvement and/or economies of scale for at least
industries in Group B.

The estimated price equations are all plausible with all coefficient estimates having the expected sign. R^2s are very high.
The level of consumption and operating and maintenance costs are
significant in all three cases. The estimated coefficients of the
fuel-cost variable, though all have a positive sign, are not significant for Group B. These results may be attributed to the fact that
fuel costs remained as a relatively stable cost component during the
sample period (the cost of fuels did not escalate dramatically until
1973). On the other hand the variable RE is significant in equations
estimated for Groups A and B. This result shows that the larger
the proportion of industrial rates, the lower the average price for
industrial customers.

Long-run own-price and cross-price elasticities as directly
derived from the estimated demand equations* are presented in
Table 2.15. As expected, the TSLS estimate of the own-price elasticity is smaller in absolute value than the LSDV estimate in all
three groups. The results show that long-run electricity demand is
price elastic in Group B, but inelastic in Group C. This difference
does not appear to be unreasonable because one would expect that the

---

is noted that one can use the price of output in place of output in an
unconstrained input demand function as derived from the profit maxi-
mization conditions. But we found this alternative specification un-
satisfactory in the present study. It is also noted that when a constrained input demand function is used, it is more appropriate to
treat output as endogenous in the model. We did not pursue this extension because the estimation of the output equation requires a detailed specification of the production function.

*The coefficients of the structural demand equation measure
the direct effects of changes in the exogenous variables on quantity
purchased. Due to the dependence of price on quantity of electricity
purchased, there will also be indirect effects on demand. For example, a decrease in output would result in a decrease in electricity
demand, which would cause average price to increase. This would,
in turn, decrease electricity demand as a result of price effect.
Estimates of the total effects of changes in the exogenous variable
on demand can be obtained by estimating the reduced-form equation.

availability of more substitutes, as is the case for Group B, would make the demand more sensitive to changes in price. For industries in Group B, the estimated elasticity with respect to price of natural gas is greater than unity, while the coal price elasticity is significant but small in magnitude.

TABLE 2.15

Estimated Direct Long-Run Price Elasticities

| Industry Group | Estimation Method | Elasticities with Respect to | | |
		Electricity Price (EP)	Gas Price (GP)	Coal Price (CP)
A	LSDV	-1.68	0.51	0.22
	TSLS	-0.90	0.52	0.28
B	LSDV	-1.60	1.02	0.32
	TSLS	-1.32	1.23	0.39
C	LSDV	-1.18		
	TSLS	-0.73		

Source: Compiled by the author.

Conclusions and Implications

Since historical data were used to estimate our industrial demand models, the results obtained in the last section characterize past relationships. Based on these estimated econometric models, it is possible to evaluate the impacts of causal factors in the past and thus their possible influence in the future.

With respect to energy conservation, it is evident that all factors except the declining price of petroleum products have contributed in a positive way to the rapid growth of electricity consumption in the past. As demand is price elastic, higher future electricity prices should result in more than proportional reduction in electricity consumption. Thus raising real price of electricity could be an effective means of conserving electricity. In reality, however, this conservation measure often cannot be implemented independent of an overall energy policy because the price of electricity usually cannot be increased alone. In fact, the changes in electricity prices usually occur as a result of changes in the prices of fuels used for electric generation. These fossil fuels are also used directly by industries.

Consider the TSLS results for the industries in Group B. If prices
of all energy fuels increase by the same percentage, electricity demand will indeed increase because the sum of the cross-price elasticities, 1.62, is greater in absolute value than the own-price elasticity. For industries in Group C, changes in prices of other energy
fuels have no impact on electricity demand. This holds, of course,
only when output can be maintained at the same level. But in reality
higher energy prices would increase the cost of producing industrial
goods which, in turn, should reduce the output demand. As a result,
output and, thus, electricity demand would both decrease.

Furthermore, in this study we have not analyzed the pattern of
interfuel substitution in great detail. This would require investigation of quantities consumed of other fuels as well as other environmental and even political factors. However, what is noteworthy is
that in Group B gas and coal are significant substitutes whereas in
Group C no significant substitutes can be identified. Furthermore,
when we conduct the analysis by grouping all industries together as
in Group A, these patterns do not adequately show up.

Finally, with respect to the impact of technological change,
our econometric demand analysis has shown that technological
change has made industries more efficient users of electricity.
Specifically, our regression results (see the coefficient of T in
Table 2.13) show that manufacturing has reduced its electricity
usage at an annual rate of 1.7 percent in Group B and 0.4 percent
in Group C as a result of improved efficiency over the period 1959-
71.* It must be noted that, after allowing for the effects of the
value deflator, these estimating rates of increasing efficiency may
appear to be a bit too high. We note, however, that because of
increasing awareness of energy problems and anticipated increases
in real price of electricity, the trends in technological change may
be accentuated in the future.

---

*In comparison, the Conference Board has shown that the
large energy users in manufacturing reduced their energy use per
unit of output between 1954 and 1967 at a rate of 1.4 percent per
year. See Conference Board, Energy Consumption in Manufacturing, a report to the Ford Foundation (Cambridge, Mass.: Ballinger,
1974).

NOTES

1. E. C. Hise and A. S. Holman, Heat Balance and Efficiency Measurements of Central, Forced-Air, Residential Gas Furnaces, Oak Ridge National Laboratory, report ORNL-NSF-EP-88, October 1975.

2. E. C. Hise, Seasonal Fuel Utilization Efficiency of Residential Heating Systems, Oak Ridge National Laboratory, report ORNL-NSF-EP-82, April 1975.

3. J. Muller and R. Bass, "An Interim Report on Some Ways of Conserving Oil," mimeographed (Washington, D.C.: Federal Energy Office, October 1, 1975).

4. David H. Nissen and David H. Knapp, "A Regional Model of Interfuel Substitution," paper presented at the SIMS Research Application Conference on Energy, Alta, Utah, July 7-11, 1975.

5. Martin L. Baughman and Paul L. Joskow, "Energy Consumption and Fuel Choice by Residential and Commercial Consumers in the United States," Massachusetts Institute of Technology, May 20, 1975.

6. For a more detailed discussion and critique of this type of logit specification, see J. S. Hausman, "Project Independence Report: An Appraisal of U.S. Energy Needs up to 1985," Bell Journal of Economics 6 (Autumn 1975): 517-51.

7. Kent P. Anderson, Residential Energy Use: An Econometric Analysis, Rand Corporation, report R-1297-NSF, October 1973.

8. A. Zellner, "An Efficient Method of Estimating Seemingly Unrelated Regressions and Tests for Aggregation Bias," Journal of the American Statistical Association 57 (June 1962): 348-68.

9. Ernst R. Berndt and David O. Wood, "Technology, Prices, and the Derived Demand for Energy," Review of Economics and Statistics 52 (August 1975): 259-68.

10. C. R. Rao, Linear Statistical Inference and Its Applications (New York: Wiley, 1965).

11. R. S. Pindyck and D. L. Rubinfeld, Econometric Models and Economic Forecasts (New York: McGraw-Hill, 1976).

12. This is true as a general tendency. But cross-section data, especially in situations where durable goods are involved, can still reflect short-run variation. See H. S. Houthakker and L. D. Taylor, Consumer Demand in the United States (Cambridge, Mass.: Harvard University Press, 1970), pp. 275-80.

13. Nissen and Knapp, op. cit.

14. Baughman and Joskow, op. cit.

15. Ibid.

16. Nissen and Knapp, op. cit.

17. Robert A. Herendeen and Clark W. Bullard III, "Energy Cost of Goods and Services, 1963 and 1967," Center for Advanced Computation, CAC Document No. 140, University of Illinois at Urbana-Champaign, November 1974.

18. Ibid.

19. Kent P. Anderson, "Residential Demand for Electricity: Econometric Estimates for California and the United States," Journal of Business 46 (October 1973): 526-53.

20. W. S. Chern, G. S. Gill, R. S. Carlsmith, and S. M. Cohn, "Electricity Demand Analysis and Forecasts for the United States," Proceedings of the Summer Computer Simulation Conference, Washington, D.C., July 12-14, 1976.

21. Franklin M. Fisher and Carl Kaysen, A Study in Econometrics: The Demand for Electricity in the United States (Amsterdam: North-Holland Publishing Company, 1962).

22. J. M. Griffin, "The Effects of Higher Prices on Electricity Consumption," Bell Journal of Economics and Management Science 5 (Autumn 1974): 515-39.

23. T. Mount, D. Chapman, and T. Tyrrell, Electricity Demand in the United States: An Econometric Analysis, Oak Ridge National Laboratory, report ORNL-NSF-EP-49, May 1973.

24. John W. Wilson, "Residential Demand for Electricity," Quarterly Review of Economics and Business 11 (Spring 1971): 7-22.

25. H. S. Houthakker, P. K. Verleger, Jr., and D. P. Sheehan, "Dynamic Demand Analysis for Gasoline and Residential Electricity Demand," American Journal of Agricultural Economics 56 (May 1974): 412-18.

26. Lester D. Taylor, Gail R. Ballenberger, and Phillip K. Verleger, Jr., "The Residential Demand for Energy," Report to the Electric Power Research Institute, June 1976.

27. Robert Halvorsen, "Demand for Electric Energy in the United States," Southern Economic Journal 42 (April 1976): 610-25.

28. Ronald P. Wilder and John F. Willenborg, "Residential Demand for Electricity: A Consumer Panel Approach," Southern Economic Journal 42 (October 1975): 212-17.

29. Wen S. Chern, "Estimating Industrial Demand for Electricity: Methodology and Empirical Evidence," in Energy: Mathematics and Models, ed. Fred Roberts, proceedings of the SIMS Conference on Energy, Alta, Utah, July 7-11, 1975; Society for Industrial and Applied Mathematics, 1976.

30. Fisher and Kaysen, op. cit.

31. John W. Wilson, "Residential and Industrial Demand for Electricity: An Empirical Analysis," Ph.D. thesis, Cornell University, 1969.

32. Taylor et al., op. cit.

33. Griffin, op. cit.

34. Houthakker and Taylor, op. cit.

35. Taylor et al., op. cit.

36. Wen S. Chern, Electricity Demand by Manufacturing Industries in the United States, Oak Ridge National Laboratory, report ORNL-NSF-EP-87, November 1975.

37. A static model, without the presence of the lagged dependent variable in the equation, was estimated for each of the selected 15 SIC three-digit industries. Results are available in ibid.

38. T. D. Wallace and Ashiq Hussain, "The Use of Error Components Models in Combining Cross Section with Time Series Data," Econometrica 37, no. 1 (January 1969): 55-68.

39. G. S. Maddala, "The Use of Variance Components Models in Pooling Cross-Section and Time Series Data," Econometrica 32, no. 2 (March 1971): 341-58.

40. M. Nerlove, "Further Evidence on the Estimation of Dynamic Economic Relations from a Time Series of Cross Section," Econometrica 39, no. 2 (March 1971): 359-82.

41. Chern, Electricity Demand, op. cit.

42. Lester Taylor, "Demand for Electricity: A Survey," Bell Journal of Economics 6 (Spring 1975): 74-110.

3

RESIDENTIAL DEMAND FOR ELECTRICITY IN THE TVA AREA

Gurmukh S. Gill
G. S. Maddala

During the first three decades of the post-World War II era, important determinants of electricity demand exhibited remarkably stable trends both in the Tennessee Valley Authority (TVA) service area and in the United States as a whole. The prices of electricity persistently declined in real terms. Population and per capita income rose steadily. The prices of substitutes for electricity such as natural gas and oil also generally declined. Starting with the late 1960s and especially during the early 1970s, this picture of stability has been changing drastically and even unpredictably. The price (average revenue per kwh) of electricity in the TVA area rose for the first time during 1967 and since then, in general, has been moving upward, especially in nominal terms (see Figure 3.1). The average changes in prices of TVA power to ultimate consumers during the period July 1967 to January 1975, as shown in Table 3.1, have been not only frequent but also substantial. The rates of

Research sponsored by the National Science Foundation RANN Program and the U.S. Energy Research and Development Administration under Union Carbide Corporation's contract with the U.S. Energy Research and Development Administration, Oak Ridge National Laboratory, Oak Ridge, Tennessee.

Programming assistance provided by S. M. Cohn is gratefully acknowledged. Assistance provided by Mary Ann Griffin and Michael Zimmer in collecting data is appreciated; also, this study benefited in part from the data gathered earlier with the help of R. D. Ellison and T. J. Tyrrell. Discussions with the TVA staff have been exceedingly helpful and the help received from the TVA's Market Analysis Branch is highly appreciated.

FIGURE 3.1

Electricity Prices and Average Annual Consumption per Residential Customer

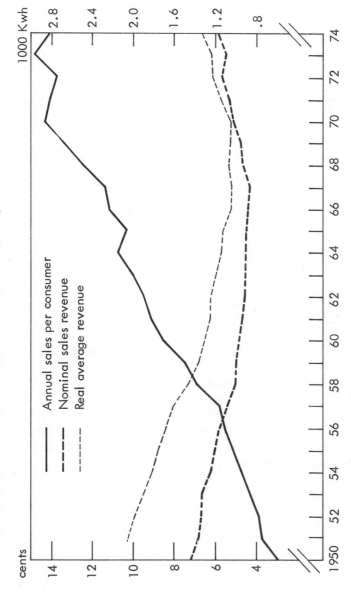

Source: Compiled by the authors.

45

increase in population and per capita real income have slowed down markedly, and the prices of substitutes for electricity have been going up. The price of oil has registered especially sharp and sudden increases.

TABLE 3.1

Average Changes in Prices (Nominal) of TVA Power
to Ultimate Consumers, July 1967–January 1975
(in percent)

Effective Date of Increase	Residential	General Power[a]	Other	Total
July 1967	8.5	5.8	3.3	6.9
March 1969	9.2	5.3	3.4	7.0
August 1969	4.7	6.0	1.9	5.2
August 1970	2.5	3.0	1.1	2.7
October 1970	19.6	22.0	9.5	20.6
January 1973	6.4	8.0	3.4	7.4
January 1974	13.5	17.7	3.5	15.6
August 1974[b]	3.1	4.1	0.9	3.7
January 1975[c]	18.3	24.8	5.7	21.9
Cumulative increase	124.0	145.5	37.5	133.9

[a]Includes directly served prevailing rate consumers.

[b]Increase based on initial amounts charged under July 1974 fuel cost adjustment addendum.

[c]Approximately one-eighth of this adjustment reflects a continuation of the July 1974 cost adjustment. Half the increase was caused by adjustments to reflect costs of purchased power.

Source: Table 3.0-1, Tennessee Valley Draft Environmental Statement, Policies Relating to Electric Power Rates (Chattanooga, Tenn., 1975).

In this period of rapid change, concern is often expressed about the stability of demand parameters estimated from historical data. The purpose of this chapter, therefore, is to examine any structural changes which may have taken place in the residential demand for electricity for the TVA service area and to illustrate the merits of disaggregated analysis in demand studies.

The sections of this chapter will give a brief description of the study area and the data used, present the models estimated, explain the results, and conclude with a summary.

SALIENT CHARACTERISTICS OF THE STUDY AREA

The TVA supplies power to 2.4 million customers through a network of 160 retail distributors. The service area covers 80,000 square miles inhabited by 6 million people in parts of seven Southeastern states. The present analysis has been confined to the customers served through TVA's local distributors, although it also serves directly 47 industrial customers with large or unusual power requirements and several federal government installations.

The TVA is the single largest electricity producer in the United States; its sales accounted for 3.4 percent of total sales and 5.8 percent of residential sales in the United States during 1971.

TVA's residential customers consume twice as much electricity per capita as the average U.S. consumer and pay only 60 percent of the average U.S. price. The level of per capita personal income is one of the lowest in the nation, yet saturation of electric appliances is one of the highest.

The study area is served by a single producer of electricity. Therefore, the empirically observed consumption of electricity can be related to a single underlying wholesale rate structure as it has varied over time, despite some variation among rates charged by retail distributors. Under this situation, TVA data are expected to yield more precise information on price–quantity relationship as compared with the results obtained from the state-level data. This expectation stems from the fact that many states are served by a number of power companies that sometimes have very divergent rate structures. Accordingly, when the average price for a state is used to represent price of electricity, much of the useful variation needed to identify price–quantity relationship gets eliminated from the data in the process of aggregation.

TVA publishes annually the electricity sales statistics by its individual retail distributors, which range in size from a single city to several counties. This permitted the use of a distributor as the unit of observation in this study. As a consequence, the study of the TVA service area escapes some of the afflictions resulting from aggregation.

The data used, units of measurement, and so on, are described in Table 3.2. The sources of data are listed at the bottom of the table. The data cover 147 distributors of TVA for the period 1962–72. The remaining distributors had to be excluded due to incomplete data.

TABLE 3.2

Description, Units of Measurement, and Sources of Data for Variables Included in Econometric Models

Description	Observed at Distributor (D), State (S), Regional (R), or National (N) Level	Symbol	Unit of Measurement	Data Sources (refer to numbered sources below)
Electricity sales	D	Q	Thousand kwh	1
Electricity sales lagged by one period	D	Q_{-1}	Thousand kwh	1
Electricity price	D	PE	Mills/kwh	1
Per capita consumer income	D[a]	PCY[b]	Thousand dollars	2-10
Residential customers	D	RC	Number	1
Heating customers	D	HC	Number	1
Gas price	S	PG	Dollars/thousand therms	11
Heating degree days	D	HD	Measured from 65° base	12
Cooling degree days	D	CD	Measured from 75° base	12
Consumer price index (all items)	N	Deflator	1970=100	13

[a]Calculated from county-level data.

[b]The TVA maintains sales and customer statistics on a fiscal-year basis; all the other data have therefore been adjusted to a fiscal-year basis.

Sources: Compiled by the authors from the following:

1. Muncipal and Cooperative Distributors of TVA Power, Annual Operations Reports, 1961-72. Chattanooga: Tennessee Valley Authority.
2. The Center for Business and Economic Research, University of Tennessee, Knoxville.
3. Bureau of Business Research, University of Mississippi, University.
4. Bureau of Population and Economic Research, University of Virginia, Charlottesville.
5. Bureau of Business Research, University of Kentucky, Lexington.
6. Bureau of Business Research, University of Alabama, Tuscaloosa.
7. Bureau of Business and Economic Research, University of Georgia, Athens.
8. School of Business Administration, University of North Carolina, Chapel Hill.
9. State of North Carolina, Department of Tax Research, Raleigh.
10. Bureau of Economic Analysis, data supplied by TVA, private communication.
11. American Gas Association, Gas Facts, 1961 to 1972.
12. Market Analysis Branch of the Tennessee Valley Authority.
13. U.S. Department of Commerce, Survey of Current Business, selected issues.

THE DEMAND MODEL

One major change that has taken place in the TVA area during the period under investigation is the phenomenal growth of electrically heated homes. In 1974, close to 40 percent of all homes were electrically heated. Given that the average consumption of an electrically heated home is about four times that of a nonelectrically heated home, the demand model we estimate must pay pointed attention to the growth in electric heating. However, since no separate breakdown of demand for heating and nonheating is available, we have to estimate a model which includes some explanatory variables (like heating degree days) that determine the demand for heating purposes.

Suppose that RC equals the total number of residential customers and HC equals the number of electric heating customers. Then

$$Q = Q_H + Q_{NH} \qquad (3.1)$$

where Q   = total quantity demanded
Q_H = demand for heating purposes
Q_{NH} = demand for nonheating purposes.

The demand for heating purposes will be a function of the number of heating customers (HC) and the rate (λ_H) at which those with electric heating will consume electricity for heating purposes:

$$Q_H = \lambda_H \times HC = \lambda_H \times \frac{HC}{RC} \times RC \qquad (3.2)$$

The proportion of heating customers HC/RC will depend on variables like income, degree of urbanization, gas availability, weather, and trends in gas and electricity prices. The rate of utilization λ_H will also depend on income, price of electricity (price of gas will not be relevant), and the number of heating degree days (HDD).

As for the demand for nonheating purposes, again a major portion of the demand will be for water heating, cooking, and clothes washing and drying, where there is a choice of what appliances to use and the rate at which appliances are utilized. The rate of utilization will depend on income and the price of electricity only, whereas the choice of what appliance to use will depend on income, gas availability, the relative trends in the prices of competing fuels, and the relative prices of different categories of appliances. Homes with electric heating would also tend to have central air conditioning, and thus their demand for electricity would also depend on the number of cooling degree days (CDD). The demand for electricity from

room air conditioners will again depend on the number of customers
having room air conditioners and the rate of utilization. The former
will depend on income and general weather conditions, and the latter
will depend on income and the number of cooling degree days in the
particular year (in addition to the price).

Attempts to model all these factors in equation 3.2 in detail
resulted in a complicated nonlinear model with a large number of
income and price terms. The estimation of this model, if feasible
in practice, would have enabled us to infer the shares of heating and
nonheating components in the total demand and also to estimate the
price and income elasticities for the different components. However,
the results were not encouraging because of the high multicollinearity among the different variables. Hence we estimated a model
where all the above factors were taken into account but in a composite way. We did not have data on the number of electrical appliances in the different areas, but we did have data on the number
of electrically heated homes. The demand function estimated was
(all variables in log form) as follows:

$$Q = \alpha_0 + \lambda Q_{-1} + \beta_1 PE + \beta_2 RC + \beta_3 \frac{HC}{RC} + \beta_4 PCY$$

$$+ \beta_5 PG + \beta_6 (HD + CD) \tag{3.3}$$

where Q_{-1} = quantity demanded in the previous year
     PE = price of electricity
     RC = number of residential customers
     HC = number of heating customers
     PCY = per capita income
     PG = price of gas
     HD = number of heating degree days
     CD = number of cooling degree days
     λ = lag coefficient.

The model in equation 3.3 assumes a simple geometric lag of
the Koyck type. More complicated lagged adjustment models like
the Solow Pascal lag, the Almon polynomial lag, or Jorgenson's
rational distributed lag could, in principle, be used, but we did not
find it worthwhile to try them. After all, we had only 12 years of
data (though over 147 cross sections). Given that we want to investigate the effects of variables such as weather and electric heating,
thus far neglected in demand studies, and to identify structural
changes that may have occurred during this period, and given also
that we have to worry about serial correlation problems, trying to
determine the shapes of the lag distribution, in addition to all these,
would have been asking too much.

We also included HD and CD as separate explanatory variables. The coefficients of both variables had the right signs (positive), and the coefficient of HD was always higher than the coefficient of CD (about three times). However, often the t ratios were not high, and hence we decided to combine the number of heating degree days and cooling degree days and included (HD + CD) as a single variable.

The prices of gas and electricity we used are average prices. For electricity we did have data on rate schedules for each of the distributors, and we could have used the marginal rates corresponding to the levels of use. However, some initial experiments revealed that this was not worthwhile. The equations using the marginal prices always had lower R^2s and gave wrong signs for some coefficients.

Equation 3.3 estimated by ordinary least squares (OLS) gave very high values of λ, thus implying very long lags in adjustment.* As is well known, the problem could be one of serial correlation in the residuals. One can account for it by assuming an autoregressive error structure in equation 3.3, but we felt that this would not get to the main source of the problem. The autocorrelation in the residuals could most probably be ascribed to omitted cross-sectional effects. Hence we decided to estimate equation 3.3 by the LSDV method (least squares with dummy variables), using cross-sectional dummies and time dummies. We also tried the variance components models (see notes 7 and 9), but very often the results were close to those obtained by the LSDV method.

As an illustration, the results for the period 1962-68 from the OLS and LSDV methods for 69 distributors with gas generally available were as follows (all variables in log form):

OLS

$$Q = 0.008 + \underset{(42.6)}{0.708} \ Q_{-1} - \underset{(-6.4)}{0.117} \ PE + \underset{(17.5)}{0.296} \ RC + \underset{(12.9)}{0.084} \ \frac{HC}{RC}$$

$$+ \underset{(5.4)}{0.045} \ PCY + \underset{(0.4)}{0.007} \ PG + \underset{(3.8)}{0.089} \ (HD + CD),$$

$$R^2 = 0.996$$

---

*In addition, the coefficient of per capita income (PCY) was almost always negative when the OLS method was used.

LSDV

$$Q = -0.235 + 0.267\ Q_{-1} - 0.551\ PE + 0.752\ RC + 0.132\ \frac{HC}{RC}$$
$$(14.6)(-13.7)(31.4)(9.2)$$

$$+ 0.075\ PCY + 0.323\ PG + 0.148\ (HD + CD),$$
$$(3.0)(3.2)(4.2)$$

$$R^2 = 0.999$$

(Figures in parentheses are t-ratios, not standard errors.)

The coefficient of the lagged dependent variable is substantially smaller (thus implying shorter lags in adjustment) and the other coefficients are substantially higher in magnitude (particularly the ones for PE and PG) when the coefficients are estimated by the LSDV method than when the coefficients are estimated by OLS. The results for the variance components model are almost identical to those of the LSDV method and hence are not presented here. This would be the case if the variance of the dummies is large relative to the error variance.[1]

There is, however, the question of whether there still remains some serial correlation bias even with the LSDV method. One cannot check this point by looking at the residuals from the LSDV equation, because of the presence of the lagged dependent variable. Hence, we estimate an extended model by introducing a first-order autoregression in the residuals, in addition to the dummies. Specifically, let U_{it} be the composite residual for the ith cross section unit in time period t. We write

$$U_{it} = U_i + V_{it} \qquad\qquad (3.4)$$

where U_i is the cross-section effect and V_{it} are residuals. In the LSDV method, we estimate U_i as constants, and in the variance component models we treat them as random variables with a common variance σ_μ^2. We now assume

$$V_{it} = \rho V_{it-1} + W_{it} \qquad\qquad (3.5)$$

If we use the LSDV model, then all we have is a regression model with lagged dependent variable and serially correlated residuals which can be handled by a nonlinear least-squares method or a search procedure (searching on ρ). If we use the variance components model, the consequence of equation 3.5 is that the successive residuals in each cross section, instead of having the same correlations, will exhibit a dampening correlation structure. The estimation of the model can again be done by searching over ρ --estimating the

variance components model with ρ-differenced data--and choosing
the value of ρ which corresponds to the maximum value of the likelihood function. Since use of this method for every model that we
considered was computationally cumbersome and expensive, we
tried it in only a couple of cases. The results showed that ρ was
close to zero, and using the formulation in equation 3.5 did not make
much difference to the final estimates. Hence, the results presented
in later sections will contain the results of estimating model 3.3 by
LSDV or the variance components method, and it would be safe to
presume that there are no further modifications that need be made in
the model to take account of serial correlation.

STRUCTURAL SHIFTS IN THE DEMAND FUNCTIONS

In principle, if we include all the variables that cause shifts in
the relationship we are estimating, then there is no need to discuss
shifts in the function. However, as mentioned earlier, a detailed
formulation in terms of equation 3.2 and the determinants of each
component of the total demand did not turn out to be amenable to
empirical estimation. Further, in the lagged adjustment model
formulated in equation 3.3, we can argue that the lag coefficient λ
will itself be a function of the rate of change of prices. For instance,
Allais[2] argued that when things are moving fast, then people make
adjustments faster than when things are moving slowly.* If we
start with the model

$$Q_t^* = X_t\beta + u_t \tag{3.6}$$

$$Q_t - Q_{t-1} = \Theta_t\,(Q_t^* - Q_{t-1})$$

where Q_t^* = the desired consumption and X_t = the set of observations
on the explanatory variables, then we get

$$Q_t = (1 - \Theta_t)\,Q_{t-1} + \Theta_t X_t\beta + \Theta_t u_t \tag{3.7}$$

---

*An opposite viewpoint would be that if things are moving fast,
people find it hard to predict the course of future events and hence
adjust slowly. In any case, a more appropriate formulation would
be that people react to the permanent components of the observed
variables, and if by moving fast we mean a high transitory component, then the reaction would be slower. The reverse will be the
case if the permanent component is changing.

and with constant Θ_t, we have the form of equation 3.3. Instead, if we assume

$$\Theta_t = \gamma + \delta \left| \frac{\dot{P}_t}{P_t} \right| \tag{3.8}$$

that is, the rate of adjustment itself is a function of the absolute value of the rate of change of prices, then this results in the equation

$$Q_t = (1 - \gamma) Q_{t-1} - \delta \left| \frac{\dot{P}_t}{P_t} \right| Q_{t-1} + \gamma X_t \beta$$

$$+ \delta \left| \frac{\dot{P}_t}{P_t} \right| X_t \beta + V_t \tag{3.9}$$

where V_t has a complicated structure. We tried to estimate equation 3.9, under the assumption that V_t are serially independent, but the results were hard to interpret--again due to multicollinearity between the variables. Hence we decided to use only equation 3.3 and test where the structural shift had taken place.

Given the behavior of the prices shown in Figure 3.1, we would expect that the shift would have occurred sometime around 1967, and also that if the above reasoning of the model in equation 3.8 is correct, the coefficient, λ, in equation 3.3 should be lower in the earlier period and higher in the later period. In fact, our results do confirm this prior reasoning.

There has been, in recent years, considerable literature on piecewise regression (see McGee and Carlton[3]) and switching regression (see Goldfeld and Quandt[4]) models to analyze structural changes. Our model is not a switching regression model with back and forth switching, and though we are talking of a piecewise regressions model with the limited data we have, we can consider only two pieces. Thus, we will postulate that there is only one switch that has occurred, and the question is to determine when. One of the commonly suggested tests for this purpose is one suggested by Brown and Durbin.[5] If β_r is the set of estimates of the regression parameters from the first observations, they essentially define successive residuals $U_r - \beta_{r-1} X_r$ for successive values of r. Using a generalization of Helmert transformation, they derive transformed residuals that are IN $(0, \sigma^2)$. They then propose testing the cumulative sums of successive residuals for significant departure from zero. In our case, with pooled cross-section and time-series data, this test is not directly applicable. Farley and Hinich suggest a test for the hypothesis that there is no switch against the hypothesis that

there is a single switch in the regression equation.[6] In our case,
we did not apply the test, because there is strong evidence that the
hypothesis of no switch would be rejected. With our data, there is
a separation of the sample period into that of falling prices and rising prices, and the question is not whether a switch has occurred
but when it occurred. We finally decided to use the Quandt method[7]
of computing the log likelihood for different partitions of the sample
(1962-67, 1968-72), (1962-68, 1969-72), and (1962-69, 1970-72)
and pick the one that gave the largest value to the log likelihood
function.

   The results for these partitions as well as for the period
1962-72 as a whole are presented in Table 3.3. The application of
the Chow tests[8] for breaks in 1967, 1968, and 1969 gave the following results:*

   A structural break in 1967: F = 5.77
   A structural break in 1968: F = 5.16
   A structural break in 1969: F = 4.07

In all cases we reject the hypothesis of no structural change. But
given the fact that we want to fix one of these years as the most
plausible year when a structural change occurred, the question is
which one of these years do we choose? The application of the
Quandt test revealed that a break in 1967 gave a higher value of the
likelihood function than a break in 1968, which, in turn, gave a
higher value of the likelihood function than a break in 1969. For the
Quandt test, we compare 723 Ln (0.4650) + 577 Ln (0.2278), 869 Ln
(0.6014) + 431 Ln (0.1225), and 1015 Ln (0.7093) + 285 Ln (0.0776).
The values are -140.71, -134.68, and -107.71. We choose the one
with the minimum value, which in this case gives 1967. An examination of the behavior of the prices shown in Figure 3.1 reveals that
this partition is reasonable even on a priori grounds.

   Given that we adopt the partitioning into the periods 1962-67
and 1968-72, the most salient features of the results in Table 3.3
are as follows:

   The adjustment is faster in the period 1962-67 than in the
period 1968-72 as revealed by the coefficient of Q_{-1}. One possible
rationalization of this result, as discussed earlier and as remarked
by Allais, is that people respond faster when things are changing

---

   *Since we have a lagged dependent variable, as one explanatory
variable, strictly speaking, the F-tests are not the right ones to
use. What we should be using are asymptotic likelihood ratio tests.
But it is clear that the conclusions will be the same.

TABLE 3.3

Demand Functions for TVA Data

	1962-68	1969-72	1962-69	1970-72	1962-67	1968-72	1962-72
Construction	0.086	-0.580	0.529	0.770	-1.037	-0.674	0.392
Q_{-1}	0.191	0.448	0.210	0.393	0.145	0.450	0.296
	(13.9)	(16.6)	(16.1)	(11.5)	(10.2)	(16.2)	(24.3)
PE	-0.544	-0.321	-0.516	-0.417	-0.491	-0.341	-0.415
	(-14.9)	(-6.4)	(-15.7)	(-5.8)	(-12.2)	(-7.8)	(-16.5)
RC	0.824	0.639	0.801	0.635	0.864	0.616	0.706
	(41.6)	(21.3)	(42.5)	(14.1)	(42.8)	(19.8)	(42.6)
HC/RC	0.140	0.111	0.150	0.164	0.164	0.111	0.162
	(12.1)	(9.1)	(14.6)	(8.4)	(13.1)	(10.7)	(20.0)
PCY	0.093	0.150	0.079	0.195	0.102	0.119	0.092
	(4.1)	(5.2)	(4.1)	(4.8)	(3.9)	(4.5)	(6.2)
PG	0.367	0.030	0.324	-0.067	0.476	0.133	0.232
	(4.0)	(0.4)	(4.1)	(-0.7)	(4.7)	(1.5)	(3.8)
HD + CD	0.111	0.104	0.069	0.068	0.160	0.115	0.091
	(3.2)	(4.1)	(2.2)	(1.8)	(4.2)	(4.3)	(3.5)
R^2	0.991	0.993	0.991	0.997	0.992	0.995	0.991
Degree of freedom	869	431	1,015	285	723	577	1,453
Residual sum of squares	0.6014	0.1225	0.7093	0.0776	0.4650	0.2278	1.1635

Source: Compiled by the authors.

fast than when things are changing slowly. During the period 1962-67 the rate of change of prices was higher (in absolute terms) than during the period 1968-72 (see Figure 3.1). In an earlier study we found the results quite opposite to the ones reported here.[9] The adjustment was faster during the period 1968-72 than during the period 1962-67. There it was argued that people responded diffrently during periods of rising and falling prices. However, the results obtained then were with preliminary data, and the current results are with revised and more accurate data. Further, the variable HC/RC was not included as an explanatory variable, and the method of estimation used there was ordinary least squares, whereas the estimation method used here is that of least squares with dummy variables (and variance components models which did not produce any significantly different results). In any case the current results which show that adjustment speeds are faster in the period 1962-67 than in the period 1968-72 are more plausible.

The income coefficient is marginally higher and the price coefficients substantially lower (particularly for natural gas) in the latter period than in the former. These results suggest that in recent years the demand for electricity is becoming more responsive to income and less responsive to price variables than in earlier years, at least in the short run. Actually one can see this more clearly if one looks at the trend in the coefficients for per capita income (PCY) and the coefficient of the price of electricity (PE) and the price of gas (PG) in the regressions for 1969-72 and 1970-72 in Table 3.3.

The long-run elasticities of demand for electricity with respect to prices, income, and number of customers for the different periods are presented in Table 3.4.

TABLE 3.4

Long-Run Elasticities

	Variable			
	PE	PG	PCY	RC
1962-68	-0.672	0.454	0.115	1.019
1969-72	-0.582	0.054*	0.272	1.158
1962-69	-0.653	0.410	0.100	1.014
1970-72	-0.687	-0.110*	0.321	1.046
1962-67	-0.574	0.557	0.119	1.011
1968-72	-0.620	0.242	0.216	1.120
1962-72	-0.589	0.330	0.131	1.003

*Not significantly different from 0.

Source: Compiled by the authors from Table 3.3.

If one looks at these long-run elasticities, one finds that those with respect to income and price of electricity are higher during recent years than in earlier years. However, the elasticities with respect to the price of gas have fallen. This is possibly a reflection of the nonavailability of gas rather than a change in price responsiveness.

Finally, it should be noted that the price and income elasticities reported here are lower than the estimates reported earlier. This is because we have the extra explanatory variable HC/RC. Both price and income variables affect this proportion in an important way. Thus, the effects reported here are the direct effects of price and income variables on electricity demand. We have to add to this the indirect effects of these variables on total demand through their effect on HC/RC. We had to include the variable HC/RC in our equations because the focus in this study has been on structural changes. Also, the fact that the income and price variables are very significant, even after the inclusion of the variable HC/RC, shows that these variables affect total demand both directly and indirectly through their effect on electric heating.

CONCLUSIONS

This chapter analyzes the residential demand for electricity in the TVA area during the period 1962-72 and considers--in addition to the commonly used explanatory variables like per capita income, price of electricity, and price of gas--variables like the proportion of heating customers, heating degree days, and cooling degree days. It is found that every one of these variables is highly significant. Also, the period 1962-67 is a time of falling electricity prices, the period 1968-72 is a time of rising electricity prices. An analysis of the relationships showed an important structural break in 1967. The analysis also shows that lags in adjustment to desired consumption levels were shorter in the former period than in the latter. This can be explained by the fact that the magnitude of price changes was higher (in absolute terms) in the former period than in the latter. Also, it has been found that in the more recent years demand has been more sensitive to income and less sensitive to prices (in the short run) than in earlier years, though the long-run elasticities (except for the price of natural gas) are higher. The perverse results for the price of natural gas are perhaps a reflection of the growing scarcity of this fuel rather than any change in consumers' price responsiveness.

NOTES

1. G. S. Maddala, "The Use of Variance Components Models in Pooling Cross Section and Time Series Data," Econometrica, March 1971, pp. 341-58.

2. M. Allais, "A Restatement of the Quantity Theory of Money," American Economic Review, December 1966, pp. 1124-57.

3. V. E. McGee and W. T. Carlton, "Piecewise Regression," Journal of the American Statistical Association, 1970, pp. 1109-26.

4. S. M. Goldfeld and R. E. Quandt, Nonlinear Methods in Econometrics (Amsterdam: North Holland Publishing Co., 1972), Chapter 9.

5. R. L. Brown and J. Durbin, "Methods of Investigating Whether a Regression Relationship Is Constant Over Time," paper presented at the European Statistical Meeting, Amsterdam, 1968.

6. J. V. Farley and M. J. Hinich, "A Test for a Shifting Slope Coefficient in a Linear Model," Journal of the American Statistical Association, 1970, pp. 1320-29.

7. R. E. Quandt, "The Estimation of a Linear Regression System Obeying Two Separate Regimes," Journal of the American Statistical Association, 1958, pp. 873-80.

8. G. C. Chow, "Tests of Equality Between Two Sets of Coefficients in Two Linear Regressions," Econometrica, 1960, pp. 561-605.

9. G. S. Gill and T. J. Tyrrell, "Demand Estimation and Forecasting Regional Electricity Demand in the Context of Rising Electricity Prices," Proceedings of the 1974 Summer Computer Simulation Conference, July 9-11, 1974, Houston, Texas, pp. 283-85.

4

ENERGY DEMAND FOR
SPACE HEATING IN
THE UNITED STATES
Wen S. Chern
William W. Lin

Space heating is the most important end use of energy in the residential sector. In 1970 space heating accounted for 56 percent of the total energy used by households (exclusive of the consumption of gasoline for transportation purposes). The purpose of this study is to develop a model of space heating demand in the residential sector for the major fuels, that is, electricity, natural gas, and petroleum products. In 1970 the space-heating consumption of energy at point of use was 6.76 quadrillion Btu, of which 54 percent was natural gas, 32 percent fuel oil, 3 percent electricity, and 11 percent others (LPG, coal, and so on). This study deals with both the utilization rate of existing stock and the fuel choice of space-heating equipment. The behavior of fuel choice (or equipment choice) was previously investigated by Anderson,[1] Baughman and Joskow,[2] Lin et al.,[3] and Wilson.[4] These studies are reviewed briefly later.

The model developed in this study consists of two parts: the first determines the average usage per heating customer, and the second deals with the proportion of occupied housing units using a particular fuel for space heating (or simply the analysis of saturation). Specifically, our study embodies the following significant features. First, our model estimates both energy utilization rate and fuel choice for space heating. The rationale for dealing with these two demand components separately is that energy demand is determined in the short run by rate of utilization of existing stock of

Research sponsored by the U.S. Energy Research and Development Administration under contract with the Union Carbide Corporation, Oak Ridge National Laboratory, Oak Ridge, Tennessee.

heating equipment and in the long run by both rate of utilization and fuel switching. Second, to our knowledge, we are among the first to include appliance prices as explanatory variables in the fuel-choice model. Lin et al also included appliance prices in their model. [5] Third, we employ marginal prices of electricity rather than the commonly used average price for both the usage and the fuel-choice equations. Fourth, the fuel-choice model does not impose a rigid constraint that cross-price saturation elasticities with respect to a given fuel price be identical. Such a restriction is necessary in the models developed by Anderson[6] and Baughman and Joskow. [7]

RATE OF UTILIZATION

Since available data on space heating consumption are not adequate for an econometric analysis, the model developed in this study includes both heating and nonheating components. The total residential consumption (Q) of a particular fuel at the state level can be expressed as

$$Q_i = \lambda_i HC_i + \beta_i NHC_i \qquad (4.1)$$

where HC_i = number of heating customers who use fuel i
NHC_i = number of nonheating customers who use fuel i
λ_i = average consumption per heating customer who uses fuel i
β_i = average consumption per nonheating customer who uses fuel i.

Consumption per heating customer may be divided into two components as

$$\lambda_i = \alpha_i + \beta_i \qquad (4.2)$$

where $_i$ is the average consumption for space heating. Note that the sum of HC_i and NHC_i equals the total number of residential customers (RC_i). Substituting equation 4.2 into equation 4.1 and dividing both sides of the equation by RC_i yields

$$Q_i/RC_i = \alpha_i(HC_i/RC_i) + \beta_i \qquad (4.3)$$

where Q_i/RC_i is the average consumption per residential customer and HC_i/RC_i is the saturation ratio of fuel i for space heating. Thus equation 4.3 decomposes the average consumption per residential customer into a space-heating and a nonspace-heating component.

We further postulate that the average consumption for heating is a function of the price of the fuel in question, personal income, and heating degree days. Also, the average consumption for non-heating purposes is assumed to be a linear function of their demand determinants, including the price of fuel, personal income, and saturation ratios of nonheating appliances. Therefore, the regression equations to be estimated are

$$Q_i/RC_i = U_i\,(\cdot)(HC_i/RC_i) + W_i\,(\cdot) \qquad\qquad (4.4)$$

where $U_i\,(\cdot)$ and $W_i\,(\cdot)$ are linear functions of the relevant demand determinants for heating and nonheating purposes, respectively. The relevant variables appearing in $U_i\,(\cdot)$ and $W_i\,(\cdot)$ differ, of course, for different fuels.

In order to estimate equation 4.4, it is necessary to have data on both the numbers of residential customers and residential heating customers for each fuel. Unfortunately, data for these two variables are not available for petroleum products. Therefore, we replace the number of residential customers and the ratio of heating customers to residential customers by the number of occupied housing units and the fraction of occupied housing units using oil for heating, respectively, in the petroleum products equation. The use of these latter two variables is not consistent with the model specified in equation 4.4. Consequently, some adjustments are needed for computing the usage elasticities, which are discussed later. Data on heating customers are also not available for electricity. As a result, we use the fraction of occupied housing units using electricity for heating in place of the ratio of heating customers to residential customers. This change should not cause any problems because every household uses electricity.

The variables used for estimating equation 4.4 are defined as follows:

E	= average electricity consumption per residential electricity customer
G	= average natural gas consumption per residential customer
O	= average oil consumption per occupied housing unit using oil for heating
SE	= the fraction of electricity customers using electricity for heating
SG	= the fraction of gas customers using gas for heating

SO   = the fraction of occupied housing units using oil for
          heating
MPEB = the marginal price of electricity measured as the
          difference between a typical electric bill (TEB) for
          750 kwh and a TEB for 1,000 kwh per month
MPEA = the marginal price of electricity measured as the
          difference between a TEB for 250 kwh and a TEB for
          500 kwh per month
PG   = average price of natural gas
PO   = retail price of No. 2 fuel oil
HDD   = heating degree days
CDD   = cooling degree days
SEWH = saturation of electric water heating measured as the
          fraction of occupied housing units using electricity
          for water heating
SEF   = saturation of electric food freezer measured as the
          fraction of occupied housing units having food freezer
STV   = saturation of television set
SGCD = saturation of gas clothes dryer
SOWH = saturation of oil water heater
Y   = per capita personal income

The above list includes only those variables kept in our final
equations. We tried essentially all saturation variables for all appliances in our preliminary testing of the model but deleted many of
them because of poor results. The units of measurement and data
sources are given in the Appendix to this chapter.

The system of the three usage equations fits the general specification used by Zellner for seemingly unrelated regressions.[8] Thus,
Zellner's generalized least squares (GLS) approach was employed to
estimate equation 4.4 for electricity, natural gas, and petroleum
products simultaneously. Cross-sectional data by state, for 1970,
were used. The final regression equations are given below:

Electricity:

$$E = 9.17 \text{ SE} - 973.8 \text{ MPEB} \times \text{SE} + 0.0041 \text{ HDD} \times \text{SE}$$
$$\quad (1.45) \quad (-2.65) \qquad\qquad (4.32)$$
$$-16.86 \text{ MPEA} + 3.453 \text{ SEWH} + 4.387 \text{ SFF}$$
$$\quad (-0.59) \qquad (5.31) \qquad\qquad (4.29)$$
$$+4.205 \text{ STV} + 0.0016 \text{ CDD} + 0.00087 \text{ Y}$$
$$\quad (0.63) \qquad (9.08) \qquad\qquad (4.02)$$
$$+5.23 \qquad\qquad R^2 = 0.97 \qquad\qquad\qquad (4.5)$$
$$(-0.82)$$

Natural gas:

$$G = 0.0876\ SG - 0.0000543\ PG \times SG$$
$$\ (5.89) \qquad\qquad (-3.33)$$
$$\ +0.0000103\ HDD \times SG + 0.1424\ SGCD + 0.0456$$
$$\ (7.05) \qquad\qquad\qquad (3.36) \qquad\qquad (2.55)$$
$$\ R^2 = 0.83 \tag{4.6}$$

Petroleum products:

$$O = 58.46\ SO - 3.412\ PO \times SO + 0.0036\ HDD \times SO$$
$$\ (2.93) \qquad (-3.24) \qquad\qquad (6.63)$$
$$\ +12.53\ SOWH + 2.118$$
$$\ (2.75) \qquad\quad (3.75)$$
$$\ R^2 = 0.92 \tag{4.7}$$

The figures in parentheses are estimated t-ratios and R^2 is the squared correlation coefficient between the actual and estimated values of the dependent variable. For each of the three estimated equations, the first three variables explain the heating component and the rest of the variables, including the constant term, explain the nonheating component.

In the electricity equation, we used the marginal price for higher blocks (MPGB) to explain the heating component and that for lower blocks (MPEA) to explain the nonheating portion of electricity usage. The results are fairly good, with all variables having the expected sign. All estimated coefficients are significant at the 5 percent level of significance except the marginal price of electricity (MPEA) and the saturation of television sets (STV) in the nonheating component.

The final equation of natural gas shows that the price of natural gas (PG) and heating degree days (HDD) are two significant factors in the heating component and the saturation of gas clothes dryer (SGCD) is the only significant factor in the nonheating component. The saturations of gas water heating and cooking and personal incomes were initially included but were later dropped because the estimated coefficients did not have the expected sign. For petroleum products, oil price (PO) and heating degree days (HDD) are significant in the heating component, and the saturation of oil water heater (SOWH) is a significant variable in the nonheating portion of the equation.

It is somewhat surprising that the income variable did not show any effect on the utilization rates of all energy sources for space heating. Income is, however, an important determinant of fuel choices as discussed later. The implication is that the level of income affects the household's decision on type of appliance to purchase but not the rate to operate it. It should be mentioned that we tried an alternative variable using the percentage of families with higher annual income ($15,000-$25,000) to investigate whether or not income distribution plays a role in determining usage rate. This variable, however, never had a significant coefficient with the correct sign.

FUEL CHOICES

Past studies attempted to estimate the proportion of residential customers choosing a particular fuel for a particular end use using different model specifications. Wilson, in his work focusing on electric appliance choices, specified the "percentage of homes with at least one unit of appliance X" as the dependent variable in the appliance market share equations.[9] He then fit these equations with both logarithmic and linear forms, sensitive to prices of electricity and gas, income and climatic conditions (heating degree days) for cooking, water heating, space heating, food freezing, and air conditioning.

While Wilson's model is straightforward and yields unique single-valued price and income saturation elasticities, it nevertheless has a shortcoming of not including oil price or equipment cost variables.

Anderson's model for predicting relative market shares of residential fuel choices involves equations of the following form:[10]

$$\ln\left(\frac{S_i}{S_j}\right) = \beta_0 + \beta_1 \ln P_i + \beta_2 \ln P_j + \beta_3 \ln Y$$
$$+ \beta_4 \ln HS + \beta_5 SHU + \beta_6 NU + \beta_7 W + U$$

where S_i = fraction of total installations that consume energy type i
P_i = price of fuel i
Y = per capita income
HS = average household size
SHU = fraction of households in single-family detached housing units
NU = fraction of households in nonurban housing units
W = mean December or July temperature
U = random error term
βs are unknown parameters.

For a given j, the above equation is estimated for each i (except for i = j). The equations are estimated jointly under the constraint that β_2 be the same in all equations. Therefore, all cross-price elasticities with respect to a given price change are identical. For instance, the cross-price elasticities of demands for natural gas and for oil with respect to electricity price are assumed to be the same. Prices of competing fuels other than i and j do not enter the equation. This specification imposes rather strong assumptions on the structure of fuel-share equations.

As noted by Anderson himself, the estimated regression coefficients for this model vary depending upon the choice of jth fuel in the denominator of the dependent variable. Therefore, the estimated price and income elasticities are not unique and occasionally show large differences. For example, in the space-heating equation the β coefficients of electricity price range from -1.05 to -3.20 and the β coefficients of income range from -1.03 to +1.65. Saturation elasticities were then computed using β coefficients that lie somewhere in the middle of the ranges.

Baughman and Joskow's appliance choice model is similar to Anderson's although a semilog rather than a log-log formulation was used.[11] Again, the appliance choice equations were estimated simultaneously under the constraint that all the cross-price β coefficients are identical for any explanatory variable j.

Recently, Lin et al. estimated a conditional logit model specified as:[12]

$$\ln\left(\frac{S_i}{1-S_i}\right) \equiv \alpha_i = \sum_{j=1}^{J} \beta_{ij} X_j + U_i$$

where i = type of fuel (i = 1,2,3,4: electricity, gas, oil, other/none)

S_i = fraction of occupied housing units that use fuel i

X_j = a set of explanatory variables including prices of major fuels (electricity, gas, fuel oil), prices of household equipment, per capita income, demographic variables and climatic variables (heating degree days, cooling degree days)

U = random error term

α and β are unknown parameters.

Their formulation improves upon the Baughman-Joskow study in that the models are less restrictive, but yield unique estimates of price and income elasticities, equipment prices are included as explanatory variables, and the models' constraint predicted market shares to lie between 0 and 1.

In this study, a linear market-shares model is used because of the simplicity of both the model interpretation and estimation. We intend to show that such a simple model in which price and income elasticities are also uniquely determined yields results similar to those obtained in more elaborate models as used by Lin et al.,[13] except that we employ marginal price rather than average price for electricity.

The three market-share equations for electricity, natural gas, and petroleum products have the following general expression:

$$S = A_{i0} + A_{i1}MPEB + A_{i2}PG + A_{i3}PO$$

$$+ A_{i4}POH + A_{i5}Y + A_{i6}HDD$$

$$i = 1, 2, 3 \tag{4.8}$$

where S_1 = fraction of occupied housing units that use electricity for heating

S_2 = fraction of occupied housing units that use natural gas for heating

S_3 = fraction of occupied housing units that use oil for heating

POH = price of oil heater

MPEB, PG, PO, Y, and HDD have been previously defined.

Under the linear specification in equation 4.8, the fact that the market shares must sum up to unity implies that

$$\sum_{i=1}^{3} A_{i0} = 1 \text{ and} \tag{4.9}$$

$$\sum_{i=1}^{3} A_{ij} = 0, \text{ for } j = 1, \ldots, 6 \tag{4.10}$$

The sum of all constant terms in the market-share equations must equal unity, and the sum of the estimated coefficients for each variable across the equations must equal zero.

The system of equations shown in equation 4.8 can best be estimated by the ordinary least-squares approach, because the same set of independent variables is used in all three equations and the OLS estimates automatically satisfy the constraints of equations 4.9 and 4.10. Data for 48 states in 1970 were used to estimate equation

4.8. The regression results are presented in Table 4.1. The over-all performance of the model is reasonably good in terms of signs and the statistical significance of the estimated coefficients.

Results show that all own-price and cross-price coefficients have the expected signs and are mostly statistically significant. The price of oil heater (POH) is significant in the equations for natural gas and petroleum products. The estimated coefficients for the POH indicate that when the POH increases, the market share of petroleum products will decrease, while shares of both electricity and natural gas will increase. With respect to income effects, the estimated coefficients do not have high t-ratios. The results, however, show that an increase in income would increase market shares for electricity and natural gas and would reduce the share for petroleum products. For heating degree days, the re-sults suggest that petroleum products are more common in colder states than are natural gas or electricity. These results are fairly similar to those obtained by Lin et al.[14]

USAGE AND SATURATION ELASTICITIES

The main objective of this study is to estimate fuel price elasticities for the usage and saturation components of space-heating demand in the residential sector. To compute usage elas-ticities, we first derive, from equations 4.5-4.7, three average usage equations for the heating component. For example, the aver-age heating usage function for electricity is obtained from equation 4.5 as

$$U_1 = 9.17 - 973.8MPEB + 0.0041HDD \qquad (4.11)$$

For electricity and natural gas, usage elasticities can be easily com-puted from the sample means of usage, fuel prices, and degree days. For petroleum products, the computation is more complicated. Be-cause of the lack of data on heating customers (HC) and residential customers (RC) of petroleum products, we have estimated the fol-lowing equation:

$$Q/OH = U^*(\cdot) \ (HC/OH) + W^*(\cdot) \qquad (4.12)$$

where OH is the total number of occupied housing units. The true average usage is $U(\cdot)$ (see equation 4.4), but $U^*(\cdot)$ was estimated in our model. However, it can be shown that

$$W^*(\cdot) = W(\cdot) \text{ and } U(\cdot) = U^*(\cdot) \ (OH/RC) \qquad (4.13)$$

TABLE 4.1

Estimated Market-Share Equations for Space Heating, 1970

Type of Fuel	Dependent Variable	Explanatory Variables							R^{2a}
		MPEB	PG	PO	POH	Y	HDD	Constant	
Electricity	S_1	-21.75 (-5.15)[b]	0.00007 (2.46)	0.0094 (1.47)	0.0001 (0.86)	0.00003 (1.16)	-0.00001 (-1.77)	-0.09 (-0.27)	0.63
Natural gas	S_2	17.13 (2.32)	-0.00054 (-10.75)	0.0089 (0.80)	0.0007 (2.85)	0.00002 (0.38)	-0.00002 (-1.55)	-0.40 (-0.77)	0.83
Petroleum products	S_3	4.62 (0.68)	0.00047 (10.19)	-0.0183 (-1.79)	-0.0008 (-3.65)	-0.00005 (-1.137)	0.00003 (2.80)	1.49 (3.09)	0.85

[a]R^2 is the multiple coefficient of determination.

[b]Figures in parentheses are t-ratios.

Source: Compiled by the authors.

where OH/RC is the reciprocal of the percentage of houses using petroleum products. Although data on OH/RC are not available, Heddleson has estimated that 24 percent of the single-family detached homes in the United States were heated by oil in 1970.[15] Since more than 90 percent of the petroleum products used in the residential sector were for heating, it is reasonable to use Heddleson's estimate as proxy for RC/OH. Therefore OH/RC = 1/0.24, which equals approximately 4.167. True mean usage of petroleum products is obtained by adjusting the computed mean by a factor of 4.167 according to equation 4.13. The usage elasticities for petroleum products are then computed from the means of adjusted usage, fuel prices, and degree days.

Saturation elasticities can be easily computed from the estimated market-share equations, using the sample means of shares, fuel prices, degree days, and income. The resulting usage and saturation elasticities are presented in Table 4.2. Since the model was estimated from cross-sectional data, the computed elasticities are generally interpreted as long-run elasticities.

TABLE 4.2

Estimated Usage and Saturation Elasticities for Space Heating[a]

Type of Fuel	Electricity Price (MPEB)	Gas Price (PG)	Oil Price (PO)	Heating Degree Days (HDD)	Income (I)
Usage Elasticities					
Electricity	-0.69	b	b	1.19	c
Natural gas	b	-0.73	b	0.68	c
Petroleum products	b	b	-0.87	0.28	c
Saturation Elasticities					
Electricity	-3.59	0.85	1.78	-0.60	1.16
Natural gas	0.46	-1.08	0.28	-0.15	0.11
Petroleum products	0.24	1.78	-1.07	0.47	-0.56

[a]Computed at sample means.

[b]No cross-price elasticities are estimated, because they are identically zero.

[c]Not estimated.

Source: Compiled by the authors.

The results show that the price elasticity of usage for all three fuels is smaller than unity. In all cases, the estimated usage elasticities are smaller than the own-price elasticities of saturation. While the cross-price elasticities are identically equal to zero in the usage equations, their magnitudes are fairly large in several cases in the market-share equations.

Table 4.3 shows the price elasticities of saturation estimated by others. By comparison, our estimate of the own-price elasticity of saturation for electricity is smaller in absolute value than that estimated by Wilson[16] but higher than those estimated by Anderson[17] and Baughman and Joskow,[18] and close to that of Lin et al.[19] The own-price elasticities of saturation for natural gas and petroleum products are similar to those reported by Lin et al. Our cross-price elasticities of saturation are generally within the range estimated by other studies.

TABLE 4.3

Fuel Price Saturation Elasticities Estimated by Others

| | Type of Fuel | | |
	Electricity	Gas	Oil
Lin et al.			
PE[a]	-3.19	0.57	-0.18
PG	0.38	-1.33	2.95
PO	1.09	0.03	-1.01
Anderson			
PE	-2.04	0.17	0.17
PG	2.21	-1.80	2.21
PO	0.55	0.55	-1.58
Baughman & Joskow			
PE	-2.08	0.23	0.23
PG	2.12	-1.48	2.12
PO	3.30	3.30	-7.21
Wilson			
PE	-4.88		
PG	1.20		
PO	b		

[a]PE = price of electricity
  PG = price of natural gas
  PO = price of oil
[b]Blanks indicate no estimates available.
Source: See text for specific references.

The sum of usage and saturation elasticities gives the total electricity for space-heating demand. The total own-price elasticity for natural gas is -1.81, and the total own-price elasticity for petroleum products is -1.94. For electricity, the total own-price elasticity appears to be much larger than estimated for the aggregate demand for all purposes. These results, therefore, imply that space-heating demand for electricity is much more sensitive to price changes than other end-use demands of electricity.

CONCLUDING COMMENTS

This study shows that energy demand for space heating can be modeled into two separate components: the short-run usage function which determines the rate of utilization of heating appliances, and the long-run fuel-choice function which characterizes the appliance ownership decisions. The results indicate that usage elasticities are generally smaller than saturation elasticities.

The average usage equations for heating are derived from the combined usage equations for heating and nonheating purposes. The fuel-choice equations are sensitive to fuel prices, equipment prices, personal income, and weather variables. The estimated own-price elasticities of saturation are greater than unity in all cases, indicating that this component of space-heating demand is price elastic in the long run.

The sum of usage and saturation elasticities gives the total demand elasticity for space heating. The results suggest that the heating demand for electricity is more price responsive than other electricity end-use demands.

The study further shows that a simple linear market-share model yields reasonable results. The estimated saturation elasticities are mostly within the range of those estimated in other more elaborate models.

APPENDIX: UNITS OF MEASUREMENT AND DATA SOURCES FOR VARIABLES

Variable	Unit of Measurement	Source*	Variable	Unit of Measurement	Source*
E	10^3 kwh	1	CDD	days	7
G	10^4 therms	2	Y	dollars	8
O	barrels	3,4	SG	percent	2
SE (S_1)	percent	3	PG	dollars/10^4 therms	2
MPEB	dollars/kwh	5	SGCD	percent	3
HDD	days	6	SO (S_3)	percent	3
MPEA	dollars/kwh	5	PO	cents/gallon	9
SEWH	percent	3	SOWH	percent	3
SFF	percent	3	S_2	percent	3
STV	percent	3	POH	dollars	10

*Numbers refer to those in list of Data Sources.

Data Sources

1. Edison Electric Institute, Statistical Yearbook of the Electric Utility Industry for 1971. New York: Edison Electric Institute, 1971.

2. American Gas Association, Gas Facts, 1970 Data. Arlington, Va.: American Gas Association, 1971.

3. U.S. Bureau of the Census, 1970 Census of Housing: Detailed Housing Characteristics, U.S. Summary. Washington, D.C.: U.S. Government Printing Office, 1970.

4. U.S. Bureau of Mines, Mineral Industry Surveys. Washington, D.C.: U.S. Government Printing Office, 1970.

5. Federal Power Commission, Typical Electric Bills. Washington, D.C.: U.S. Government Printing Office, December 1970.

6. National Climatic Center, U.S. Department of Commerce, "Monthly Heating Degree Days by State and Season, 1931-1973." Asheville, N.C. (Job No. 14624), November 1973.

7. National Oceanic and Atmospheric Administration, U.S. Department of Commerce, Climatological Data: National Summary, 1971. Washington, D.C.: U.S. Government Printing Office, 1971.

8. U.S. Bureau of the Census, Statistical Abstract of the United States, 1973. Washington, D.C.: U.S. Government Printing Office, 1974.

9. U.S. Department of Agriculture, Agricultural Prices, 1970 Annual Summary. Washington, D.C.: U.S. Government Printing Office, 1974.

10. J. Delene, A Regional Comparison of Energy Resource Use and Cost to Consumer of Alternate Residential Heating Systems, ORNL/TM-4688, November 1974.

NOTES

1. Kent P. Anderson, Residential Energy Use: An Econometric Analysis (Santa Monica, Calif.: Rand Corporation, 1973).

2. M. Baughman and P. Joskow, "The Effects of Fuel Prices on Residential Appliance Choice in the United States," Land Economics 51 (February 1975): 41–69.

3. William Lin, Eric Hirst, and Steve Cohn, Fuel Choices in the Household Sector, ORNL/TM-5593 (1976).

4. John W. Wilson, "Residential Demand for Electricity," Quarterly Review of Economics and Business 1 (Spring 1971): 7–27.

5. Lin et al., op. cit.

6. Anderson, op. cit.

7. Baughman and Joskow, op. cit.

8. A. Zellner, "An Efficient Method of Estimating Seemingly Unrelated Regressions and Tests for Aggregation Bias," Journal of the American Statistical Association 57 (June 1962): 348–56.

9. Wilson, op. cit.

10. Anderson, op. cit.

11. Baughman and Joskow, op. cit.

12. Lin et al., op. cit.

13. Ibid.

14. Ibid.

15. F. A. Heddleson, Fuels Used for Single-Family Detailed Residential Heating in the United States, ORNL/TM-4690 (March 1975).

16. Wilson, op. cit.

17. Anderson, op. cit.

18. Baughman and Joskow, op. cit.

19. Lin et al., op. cit.

CHAPTER

5

THE GROWTH OF ELECTRIC HEATING IN THE TVA AREA

Gurmukh S. Gill
G. S. Maddala
Steve M. Cohn

Electric heating is potentially the most important source of growth in residential electricity demand. The average amount of electricity used in an electrically heated home is about four times the amount used in a nonelectrically heated home. Electric heating accounts for about 50 percent of the total electricity used in an electrically heated home. In 1974, in the TVA area, the average annual use was 14,500 kilowatt hours, and since nearly 40 percent of the homes were electrically heated, one might expect that approximately 35 percent of total residential demand was due to electric heating. The average residential use in 1974 was less than that in 1973, which was 15,000 kwh. Part of this decline can be attributed to the decreased demand for electric heating since the winter of 1973-74 was 19 percent warmer than the preceding winter. Thus, electric heating is not only an important source of electricity-demand growth but is also an important source of fluctuation in this demand due to changing weather conditions. Further, by contributing to winter peak demand, electric heating might contribute proportionately more to TVA's capacity needs than nonheating uses of electric power.

Research sponsored by the National Science Foundation RANN Program under Union Carbide Corporation's contract with the U.S. Energy Research and Development Administration, Oak Ridge National Laboratory, Oak Ridge, Tennessee.

We thank Roger Carlsmith, Wen Chern, and Charles Kerley for their careful reviews of this report. Assistance provided by Mary Ann Griffin and Michael A. Zimmer in collecting data is appreciated; also data gathered earlier with the help of Ray D. Ellison and T. J. Tyrrell were beneficial to this study.

K. P. Anderson[1] and National Economic Research Associates
(NERA)[2] have previously studied the importance of electric heating
in residential electricity consumption. They used cross-section
data for 48 states in the year 1970. The present study analyzes
data for the TVA area, where the proportion of electrically heated
homes is much higher than elsewhere in the nation* and where we
had data for the last 14 years. Table 5.1 incorporates the data for
the ratio of customers using electric heat to total residential electrical customers for the TVA area as a whole, both including and excluding Memphis; the table also gives data for the cooperative and
municipal retail distributors separately. The last two columns tend
to show rural and urban differences in the use of electric heating.
Figure 5.1 shows the growth of electric heating in these areas. The
growth curves during this period exhibit a trend which is nearly
linear, and in spite of some recent rate increases for electricity in
the TVA area, the growth of electrically heated homes does not show
signs of slowing down. If one were to attempt any projections for
the future based on these data, one would have to use an extrapolation of the linear trend. For instance, based on the figures for the
TVA area excluding Memphis, the projected proportion for 1985
would be around 54.8 percent. A more logically appealing estimate
would be obtained by extrapolating on the basis of a logistic trend
equation. The advantage of a logistic is that it recognizes that the
proportion is constrained, by definition, to lie between 0 and 1. In
contrast, with the linear trend equation, the projection could theoretically fall outside this range, giving an illogical result, although
in this case it did not. Also, the logistic permits the estimation of
a ceiling proportion--the proportion of homes that eventually will
be using electric heating. It is doubtful, however, that good estimates of the ceiling and other parameters of the logistic could be
obtained when all the data points fall in the middle (almost linear)
portion of the logistic growth curve.

The purpose of this study is to analyze the more detailed data
by distributors that TVA publishes in its annual reports and to obtain
both a better understanding of the growth in electric heating and a
projection of future heating demand based on major determinants,

---

*Almost 40 percent of the homes in the TVA area are heated
electrically. In the East Southcentral region (of which the TVA service area constitutes an important part) this proportion was only 20
percent in 1970. In contrast, the neighboring West Southcentral
census region had only 4 percent electrically heated homes. South
Atlantic and Pacific states claimed, respectively, 13 percent and 10
percent electrically heated homes. This proportion in all the other
regions was well below 10 percent.

rather than a simple extrapolation of the trend equations, linear or logistic. The extrapolation procedure is less useful, because it fails to provide useful clues needed by power planners or policy makers for understanding the rapid spread of electric heating.

TABLE 5.1

Proportion of Electrically Heated Homes in
the TVA Area from 1961 through 1974

| | Total for TVA Area | | | Municipalities |
Year	Excluding Memphis	Including Memphis	Cooperatives	Excluding Memphis
1961	0.227		0.130	0.292
1962	0.247		0.152	0.310
1963	0.260		0.168	0.320
1964	0.275		0.185	0.333
1965	0.287	0.257	0.198	0.345
1966	0.299	0.268	0.209	0.357
1967	0.310	0.278	0.219	0.368
1968	0.321	0.288	0.245	0.380
1969	0.336	0.303	0.245	0.394
1970	0.349	0.316	0.259	0.406
1971	0.358	0.326	0.273	0.413
1972	0.368	0.336	0.290	0.419
1973	0.384	0.351	0.309	0.433
1974	0.401	0.367	0.330	0.449

Source: Compiled by the authors.

The second section of this chapter presents the estimates and an analysis of the logistic equations for the individual distributors. The third section presents some equations explaining the proportions of electric heating in different years. The fourth section deals with the forecast of future demand based on the different equations estimated, and the final section presents the conclusions.

LOGISTIC GROWTH CURVES

Although the aggregate data given in Table 5.1 and plotted in Figure 5.1 exhibit such smooth trends, there are variations in both

FIGURE 5.1

Proportion of Electrically Heated Homes in the TVA Area, 1961–74

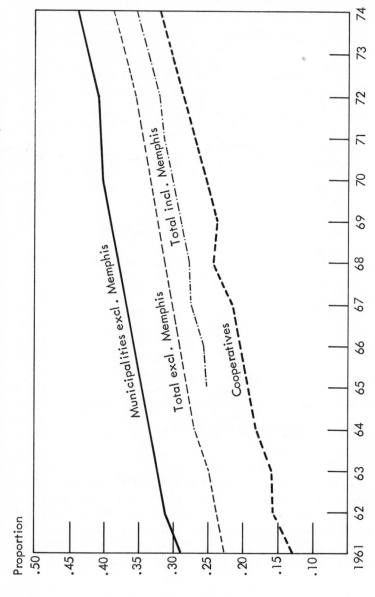

Source: Compiled from TVA annual reports.

the levels and rates of growth in electric heating among the distributors. Tables 5.2 and 5.3 present the proportions and parameter
estimates for a few major cities, and Figure 5.2 shows the corresponding graphs. The purpose of this chapter is to explain these
differences in terms of the pertinent economic determinants such as
per capita income, price and availability of gas, price of electricity,
dummy variables such as weather (based on the number of heating
degree days), and whether the distributor primarily serves a metropolitan area, town, or rural area.

Though the heating proportion curves in Figure 5.2 did not
closely resemble a logistic growth curve, an attempt was made to
summarize the data for the 144 distributors (for which we had data
from 1962 to 1974) by the parameters of the logistic growth curve
that best approximated the observed data. The equation estimated
was:

$$P_t = \frac{C}{1 + Be^{-At}}, \quad B > 0, \ A > 0, \ 0 < C < 1 \tag{5.1}$$

where $P_t = \dfrac{\text{number of electric heating customers}}{\text{total number of residential electric customer}}$

As $t \to \infty$, $P_t \to C$. C is called the ceiling, and the greater the value
of A, the faster the approach to the ceiling. Also,

$$\frac{dP_t}{dt} = \frac{A}{C} P_t (C - P_t)$$

Thus, the rate of growth at any time is proportional to the level already achieved and the remaining distance to the ceiling. It is this
property of the logistic that makes it attractive in the analysis of
several phenomena of growth.

Oliver has discussed several methods for estimating the logistic; he finds the method of nonlinear least squares to be most satisfactory.[3] In this method the parameters C, B, and A are estimated
by minimizing

$$Q = \sum \left(P_t - \frac{C}{1 + Be^{-At}} \right)^2 \tag{5.2}$$

To start the iterations, initial estimates of the parameters are
needed. If C is known, equation 5.1 implies

TABLE 5.2

Proportion of Electrically Heated Homes in Six Major Cities in the TVA Region

Year	Chattanooga	Nashville	Knoxville	Distributor Huntsville	Greenville	Johnson City	Memphis
1962	0.550	0.416	0.388	0.162	0.260	0.307	
1963	0.567	0.439	0.404	0.185	0.280	0.330	
1964	0.570	0.456	0.413	0.235	0.299	0.350	
1965	0.582	0.476	0.417	0.270	0.316	0.368	0.0125
1966	0.592	0.492	0.447	0.291	0.326	0.385	0.0159
1967	0.606	0.500	0.472	0.309	0.329	0.394	0.0211
1968	0.622	0.515	0.511	0.312	0.368	0.401	0.0290
1969	0.644	0.519	0.521	0.318	0.383	0.415	0.0402
1970	0.662	0.525	0.558	0.320	0.386	0.421	0.0562
1971	0.662	0.541	0.562	0.324	0.393	0.424	0.0680
1972	0.671	0.541	0.562	0.335	0.399	0.435	0.0774
1973	0.685	0.551	0.576	0.339	0.405	0.450	0.0881
1974	0.698	0.567	0.615	0.350	0.409	0.465	0.0974

Source: Compiled by the authors.

FIGURE 5.2

Proportion of Electrically Heated Homes in Six Major Cities
in the TVA Region, 1962-74

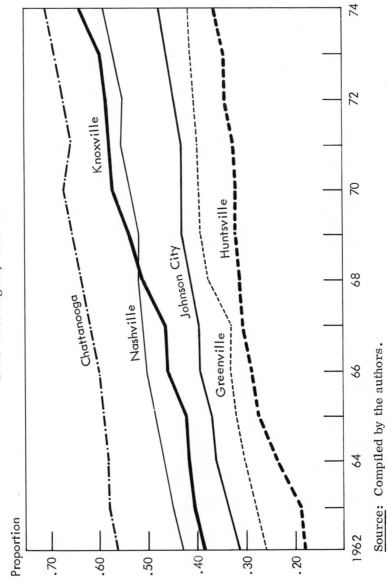

Source: Compiled by the authors.

$$\log \frac{P_t}{C - P_t} = -\log B + At \qquad (5.3)$$

and we can estimate B and A by a least-squares procedure. We obtained the estimates of C, B, and A by the nonlinear least-squares procedure, using the Newton-Raphson method of iteration. For the initial values we used some guesses of C based on the values of P_t for 1974 and 1962, and then estimated B and A from equation 5.3. For those cases for which the Newton-Raphson method did not converge, we used a search procedure to get estimates of C, B, and A. In each case, we computed a pseudo R^2 which is defined as the minimum value of Q in equation 5.2 divided by $\Sigma (P_t - \overline{P})^2$, where $\overline{P}$ is the mean of P_t. This, however, is not a satisfactory measure of the goodness of fit in this case. In many cases we found that, while the pseudo R^2 was very high, the estimates of the parameters, particularly the ceiling C, had very high standard errors. The problem essentially is that it is not possible to estimate the ceiling accurately when the only available observations are those in the middle (almost linear) portion of the logistic--which was almost always the case with the data we had.

TABLE 5.3

Estimates of Parameters for Logistic and Trend Equations
for Six Major Cities in the TVA Region

Distributor or City	$\hat{C}$	$\hat{A}$	R_p^2	$\hat{\alpha}$	$\hat{\beta}$	R^2
Chattanooga	0.883	0.070	0.987	0.535	0.0126	0.987
Nashville	0.643	0.106	0.983	0.423	0.0115	0.960
Knoxville	0.797	0.106	0.973	0.360	0.0194	0.972
Huntsville	0.472	0.125	0.940	0.191	0.0139	0.825
Greenville	0.506	0.120	0.971	0.261	0.0128	0.950
Johnson City	0.580	0.115	0.985	0.313	0.0118	0.965

Note: $\hat{C}$ and $\hat{A}$ are estimated parameters in equation 2.1 for the logistic (the estimates of $\hat{\beta}$ are not reported). R_p^2 is the pseudo R^2 for the logistic model defined in the text. $\hat{\alpha}$ and $\hat{\beta}$ are estimated parameters of the linear trend equation $P_t = \alpha + \beta t$. R^2 is the coefficient of multiple correlation for the trend equation.

Source: Compiled by the authors.

Electric heating has nowhere reached saturation levels. Even in Chattanooga, where the proportion in 1974 was as high as 70 percent, the growth curve toward the end does not show any tapering off as expected in a logistic. Thus, even though the pseudo R^2s we obtained were high (for 71 of the 144 distributors the R^2 was greater than 0.95 and for only 15 cases the R^2 was less than 0.80), the estimates of the parameters of the logistic were not good. Our purpose initially was to summarize the data in terms of the ceiling C and rate of growth A of the logistic and then to explain the differences in terms of some explanatory variables (as Griliches did in his study on the spread of hybrid corn[4]). However, the problem which presents itself in our study is that the ceiling itself could shift for each distributor due to changing economic conditions (like changes in gas availability). If the observations we have are those corresponding to a shifting logistic, then it would be difficult to give a meaningful interpretation to the differences in the estimates of the parameters of the logistic. In some cases, we noticed that the growth curve exhibited a pattern resembling that in the latter portion of a logistic, showing some signs of tapering off when suddenly, in 1974, the curve turned up (due probably to change in gas availability).

With the above-mentioned qualifications in mind, we estimated the logistic equation for 144 distributors as well as linear trend equations of the form

$$P_t = \alpha + \beta t \tag{5.4}$$

and tried to explain the parameters C and A in the logistic equation 5.1 and α and β in the linear trend equation 5.4 in terms of per capita income (PCY), gas availability (G), and a dummy variable (D) which was 0 for cooperatives and 1 for municipalities. Per capita income is taken to be the figure for 1972. Gas availability (G) is defined as the ratio of gas customers to electric heating customers (G = 0 for those distributors for which gas is not available), and the figure is taken as the average for 1969 to 1972. While both the measures are admittedly ad hoc in nature, further refinements were not considered worthwhile. More satisfactory definitions of the variables will be found in the analysis of the next section, where yearly data for individual distributors were analyzed. Table 5.4 presents the results of the regressions of α, β, C, and A on the above-mentioned explanatory variables. We had data on gas prices for only 54 of the distributors. Hence the price ratio (price of gas/price of electricity) was used as an explanatory variable for only these 54 distributors. We used both the ratios of marginal and average prices, but the average price ratio proved to be more

TABLE 5.4

Explanation of the Parameters from the Linear
and Logistic Trend Equations

---

144 Distributors

$C = 0.499 + 0.0243 \ PCY - 0.0284 \ G + 0.0058 \ D$ $R^2 = 0.2476$
    (8.6)   (1.2)   (-6.6)   (0.5)

$A = 0.1431 - 0.0093 \ PCY + 0.0022 \ G - 0.0148 \ D$ $R^2 = 0.1513$
    (7.5)   (-1.4)   (1.5)   (-4.1)

$\alpha = -0.845 + 0.0807 \ PCY - 0.0221 \ G + 0.0545 \ D$ $R^2 = 0.3893$
    (-1.5)   (4.3)   (-5.4)   (5.3)

$\beta = 0.0141 - 0.0002 \ PCY - 0.0006 \ G - 0.0016 \ D$ $R^2 = 0.1933$
    (6.8)   (-0.2)   (-3.7)   (-4.1)

101 Distributors with Gas Available

$C = 0.5020 + 0.0208 \ PCY - 0.0311 \ G + 0.0233 \ D$ $R^2 = 0.3939$
    (8.5)   (1.0)   (-7.5)   (2.0)

$A = 0.1330 - 0.0055 \ PCY + 0.0027 \ G - 0.0179 \ D$ $R^2 = 0.2269$
    (6.8)   (-0.8)   (2.0)   (-4.5)

$\alpha = 0.0853 + 0.0839 \ PCY - 0.0245 \ G + 0.0575 \ D$ $R^2 = 0.5151$
    (-1.5)   (4.4)   (-6.3)   (5.1)

$\beta = 0.0144 - 0.0003 \ PCY - 0.0006 \ G - 0.0013 \ D$ $R^2 = 0.2220$
    (6.6)   (-0.4)   (-4.0)   (-2.9)

54 Distributors with Gas Prices Available

$C = 0.2129 + 0.0463 \ PCY - 0.0006 \ D - 0.0224 \ G + 0.2111 \ PRA$ $R^2 = 0.5813$
    (2.1)   (.19)   (-0.03)   (-4.6)   (2.5)

$A = 0.1889 - 0.0109 \ PCY - 0.0080 \ D + 0.0010 \ G - 0.0438 \ PRA$ $R^2 = 0.2357$
    (5.3)   (-1.2)   (-1.1)   (0.6)   (-1.4)

$\alpha = -0.3834 + 0.1146 \ PCY + 0.0220 \ D - 0.0149 \ G + 0.2124 \ PRA$ $R^2 = 0.6976$
    (-4.4)   (5.2)   (1.3)   (-3.5)   (2.9)

$\beta = 0.0109 - 0.0004 \ PCY - 0.0007 \ D - 0.0005 \ G + 0.0027 \ PRA$ $R^2 = 0.2040$
    (2.8)   (-0.4)   (-1.0)   (-2.5)   (0.8)

Note: Figures in parentheses are t-ratios.

Source: Compiled by the authors.

satisfactory as an explanatory variable. The variable PRA finally
reported in the equations in Table 5.4 is defined as

$$\text{PRA} = \frac{1}{2} \left(\frac{\text{average price of gas in '69}}{\text{average price of elec. in '69}} + \frac{\text{average price of gas in '73}}{\text{average price of elec. in '73}} \right)$$

The years 1969 and 1973 were selected because these were the years
for which we had gas price data for the maximum number of distributors. Again, further refinements in the definitions can be made,
and by filling in the data, the analysis can be extended to cover more
distributors. However, we did not feel that these efforts would lead
to any substantial improvement in the results reported in Table 5.4.
On the basis of available data for 54 distributors, the results in
Table 5.4 show that in both the equations for the ceiling (C) estimated from the logistic and the intercept term α estimated from the
linear trend equation (which is nothing but the proportion of electrically heated homes in the first presample period 1961), the coefficients of PCY, G, and the average price ratio of gas to electricity
(PRA) are of the right sign and are significant. However, in neither
of the equations for the rate of growth, β, in the linear trend equation and the rate of growth, A, in the logistic are any of these coefficients significant.

Though the results of the above analysis are in the right direc-
tion, their use for making any demand projections appears limited.
If the relative economic conditions (for example, gas availability,
growth rate of gas and electricity prices) among the distributors
were to be stable and if the logistic growth curve fitted the observed
data well, we could have tried to explain the ceilings and rates of
growth in terms of differences among the distributors in the explanatory variables and used these results to make appropriate adjustments in the projection of demand obtained by fitting a logistic
trend equation to the aggregate data. As it stands, it is not clear
whether the logistic functions are stable, nor are the estimates of
the parameters from the logistic very good (in spite of the high
pseudo R^2s). For these reasons, as was done by Anderson and
NERA, we decided to analyze the individual proportions for each of
the years, and these results are presented in the next section.

ANALYSIS OF PROPORTIONS

In the terminology of utility companies, this is commonly
called the analysis of "saturation ratios," but we reserve this term
for the analysis of the ceiling proportions for the logistic presented
in the previous section. If the economic variables mentioned earlier

like gas availability, relative prices of gas and electricity, and income are changing at different rates in the different areas, then a more satisfactory analysis than the one presented in the previous section is the one based on an analysis of the proportions in each year. The problem we faced was that continuous data on all the variables were not available for all the distributors. There were only 32 distributors for which we had continuous data on all the variables for 11 years, 1962 to 1972. These 32 distributors accounted for 41 percent of the total number of customers with electric heating, 30 percent of the total number of residential electric customers, and 44 percent of the total number of gas customers in the area (all figures excluding Memphis). For these 32 distributors, we estimated linear probability and logit equations* of the form

$$P = \alpha_0 + \alpha_1 \ln Y + \alpha_2 \ln PG + \alpha_3 \ln PE + \alpha_4 G$$

$$+ \alpha_5 D + \alpha_6 W \tag{5.5}$$

$$\ln \frac{P}{1 - P} + \beta_0 + \beta_1 \ln Y + \beta_2 \ln PG + \beta_3 \ln PE$$

$$+ \beta_4 G + \beta_5 D + \beta_6 W \tag{5.6}$$

where P $\quad = \dfrac{\text{number of electric heating customers}}{\text{total number of residential electric customers}}$

Y $\quad$ = per capita income
PG = average price of gas
PE = average price of electricity
G $\quad$ = an index of gas availability defined as

$$\frac{\text{number of residential gas customers}}{\text{number of residential electric customers}}$$

---

*The term logit is from Berkson who wrote extensively in statistical journals on this subject in the 1950s and owes its name to the relationship with the logistic function. For example, the logistic function

$$P = \frac{1}{1 + e^{-\beta_0} X^{-\beta_1}}$$

can be transformed into the logit function

$$\ln \frac{P}{1 - P} = \beta_0 + \beta_1 \ln X$$

D = a dummy variable = 1 for metropolitan areas
                     = 0 for others
W = a weather variable
  = 1 for distributors where the weather is similar to that in
    Huntsville and Memphis
  = 0 for distributors where the weather is similar to that in
    Knoxville, Nashville, or Chattanooga.*

Since the explained variable is the proportion of homes with electric
heating, we felt that instead of using the actual number of heating
degree days, we should be using an average over a number of years.
If the explained variable were the quantity of electricity demanded,
then the number of heating degree days in that particular year would
be the appropriate explanatory variable.

In equations 5.5 and 5.6, we would expect the coefficients of
ln Y and ln PG to be positive and the coefficient of ln PE to be negative. Moreover, the coefficient of ln PE is expected to be higher in
absolute value than the coefficient of ln PG. This is easy to see if
the equations are written in terms of ln (PG/PE) and ln PE. The
coefficient of the relative price variable, ln (PG/PE), is expected
to be positive, and the coefficient of ln PE is expected to be negative.

It is customary to choose the functional form equation 5.6
instead of equation 5.5, because equation 5.5 can theoretically lead
to predictions of P outside the admissible range (0,1), whereas the
predictions from equation 5.6 will always lie in the admissible
range. We did not find this a persuasive argument in favor of equation 5.6, since for the range of data in our sample this problem did
not arise, even if projections were made as far into the future as
1990 for any reasonable assumptions about the behavior of the explanatory variables. Actually, what we found wrong with equation
5.5 was that, while it gave the right signs for all the coefficients,
the coefficient of ln PE was always less in absolute value than the
coefficient of ln PG. Also, the standard errors of the coefficients
were much higher than was the case with equation 5.6. For these
reasons, we preferred the functional form 5.6 to 5.5 and report
these results here.

---

*Data on heating degree days are available for only these
cities. When the number of heating degree days was added up for
the six years, 1968 through 1973, the results were 22,575 for Chattanooga, 22,674 for Knoxville, 22,194 for Nashville, 20,003 for
Huntsville, and 19,867 for Memphis. Hence the weather variable
was defined as a single (0,1) dummy.

Ideally, what we should be estimating is not equation 5.6 but the equation

$$\ln \frac{P}{C - P} = \delta_0 + \delta_1 \ln Y + \delta_2 \ln PG + \delta_3 \ln PE + \delta_4 G$$

$$+ \delta_5 D + \delta_6 W \qquad\qquad (5.7)$$

where C is the ceiling for the distributor. This is because equation 5.6, which is derived from an underlying logistic curve, implicitly assumes that eventually everyone will be using electric heating. Hence we estimated equation 5.7, using the ceiling proportions estimated from the previous section. The results, however, were not much different from those obtained from the estimation of equation 5.6.

To economize on space, we will present the results of estimation only for equation 5.6. These results for each of the years 1962-72 are presented in Table 5.5. It can easily be seen that the coefficients of the price variables and the gas availability variable are significant and of the right sign in all the equations. The income variable always has the right sign but has a significant coefficient only in some years. However, the persistently negative (and significant) coefficient for the weather variable W requires explanation. This variable was defined to be 1 for the distributors which have a weather similar to that in Memphis and Huntsville, and 0 for others. The coefficient may be interpreted to say that the proportion of electrically heated homes will be higher in relatively more extreme climates than in milder climates, after allowing for the effect of the other relevant variables such as gas availability, prices of electricity and gas, and per capita income. It is often thought that the proportion of electrically heated homes is likely to be lower in those areas where the climate is more extreme than in milder climates. But implicit in this thinking is the fact that the operating cost differential between an electrically heated home and a nonelectrically heated home is higher the more extreme the climate. However, we have included all the relevant price and income variables as well as an index of gas availability. In view of this, the coefficient for W would be expected to be close to zero. One possible explanation for its persistently negative and significant coefficient is that the explanatory variables included (particularly the index of gas availability) are overdoing their job. What our results suggest is that after making an allowance (possibly an over-allowance) for all these effects, the probability of having an electrically heated home is higher in extreme climates than in milder climates. Also, given that the climatic differences between the

TABLE 5.5

Analysis of Proportions

(Dependent variable = $\ln\left[\dfrac{P}{1-P}\right]$)

Year	Constant	ln Y	ln PG	ln PE	G	D	W	R^2
1962	6.562	0.4247	1.773	-3.247	-1.117	-0.1338	-0.6656	0.9064
	(3.9)	(0.7)	(2.1)	(-4.7)	(-2.5)	(-0.4)	(-2.6)	
1963	6.045	0.7348	2.113	-3.124	-0.9794	-0.0021	-0.5779	0.9208
	(3.9)	(1.5)	(2.6)	(-4.9)	(-2.4)	(-0.1)	(-2.6)	
1964	6.228	0.3692	1.890	-3.096	-1.055	-0.0795	-0.6359	0.8923
	(3.4)	(0.6)	(2.4)	(-4.2)	(-2.6)	(-0.2)	(-2.6)	
1965	5.010	0.7438	1.933	-2.681	-1.065	-0.1031	-0.5816	0.9047
	(2.8)	(1.5)	(3.3)	(-3.7)	(-3.1)	(-0.4)	(-2.8)	
1966	4.800	0.8742	1.737	-2.650	-1.164	-0.1943	-0.4370	0.8875
	(2.4)	(1.7)	(2.7)	(-3.3)	(-2.9)	(-0.6)	(-2.1)	
1967	4.297	0.9996	0.9730	-2.377	-1.685	-0.6912	-0.3343	0.8582
	(2.0)	(1.7)	(1.5)	(-2.7)	(-4.0)	(-2.2)	(-1.4)	
1968	6.754	0.5863	1.203	-3.274	-1.499	-0.6007	-0.4833	0.8615
	(2.9)	(1.0)	(1.9)	(-3.6)	(-3.6)	(-1.8)	(-2.0)	
1969	5.467	0.6145	1.466	-2.653	-1.470	-0.5962	-0.5197	0.8692
	(2.2)	(1.0)	(2.2)	(-2.8)	(-3.6)	(-1.9)	(-2.2)	
1970	4.109	0.6882	1.407	-1.962	-1.631	-0.6634	-0.4463	0.8506
	(1.5)	(1.0)	(2.1)	(-2.0)	(-4.2)	(-2.2)	(-2.0)	
1971	4.729	1.010	1.383	-2.312	-1.461	-0.4540	-0.4598	0.8767
	(1.7)	(1.7)	(2.6)	(-2.4)	(-4.6)	(-2.0)	(-2.6)	
1972	5.357	1.169	0.5217	-2.561	-1.711	-0.5765	-0.3756	0.8748
	(2.0)	(2.3)	(0.8)	(-2.8)	(-5.7)	(-2.6)	(-2.4)	

Note: Figures in parentheses are t-ratios. Each cross-sectional regression contained 32 observations.

Source: Compiled by the authors.

cities in our sample are not significantly large, an alternative explanation is that this dummy variable is picking up the effect of an important omitted explanatory variable (or variables). We have not been able to identify this variable (or variables), but since the coefficient of this dummy variable, W, is reasonably stable, we feel confident in including it in making our projections.

For the purposes of projections, we estimated pooled regression equations of the form 5.5 and 5.6, allowing for a trend term and deflating the income and price variables by a price index (for which we used the consumer price index for the United States as a whole). The pooled equations were (t-ratios in parentheses):

$$P = 0.658 + 0.1703 \ln Y + 0.3081 \ln PG - 0.1567 \ln PE$$
$$\quad (3.3) \quad (6.0) \qquad\quad (9.7) \qquad\qquad (-4.8)$$

$$- 0.2377 G - 0.1112 D - 0.0761 W + 0.00626 t,$$
$$(-12.4) \qquad (-7.3) \qquad (-6.9) \qquad (3.2)$$

$$R^2 = 0.8515 \quad (5.8)$$

$$\ln \frac{P}{1-P} = 3.902 + 0.9704 \ln Y + 1.521 \ln PG$$
$$\qquad\quad (3.6) \quad (5.9) \qquad\quad (8.2)$$

$$- 1.644 \quad PE - 1.383 G - 0.5527 D$$
$$(-8.6) \qquad\quad (-12.3) \quad (-6.2)$$

$$- 0.4741 W + 0.004844 t, \qquad R^2 = 0.8610 \quad (5.9)$$
$$(-7.3) \qquad (4.2)$$

Though the R^2 and the t-ratios are high, equation 5.8 for P cannot be used for prediction, because the coefficient of ln PE is less in absolute value than the coefficient of ln PG. Thus, if we consider two situations (other things being equal):

Situation A: PE goes up 10 percent, PG goes up 20 percent
Situation B: PE goes up 37.5 percent, PG goes up 50 percent

so that the relative price PG/PE is the same in both cases, then equation 5.8 will predict a greater percentage of electrically heated homes in situation B.* It is, however, interesting to note that the

---

*We would expect changes in the relative price PG/PE to cause a shift in the demand curve for electric heating. With the relative price PG/PE remaining constant, an electricity own-price

trend term in equation 5.8 is 0.00626, which is about half of what it would be if the explanatory variables had not been included. In any case, for purposes of prediction, we will be using equation 5.9.

PROJECTIONS OF GROWTH IN ELECTRIC HEATING

The projections of the proportion of electrically heated homes as obtained by straight trend projections and by the use of the estimated equation 5.9, where the effects of income and price variable are taken into account, will now be compared. The proportion of electrically heated homes (for all distributors in the area excluding Memphis) was 0.227 in 1962 and 0.401 in 1974. Based on the data reported in Table 5.1, the projection obtained by a linear trend is 54.8 percent in 1985. If we use a logistic trend, the corresponding projection for 1985 [with no ceiling estimated, that is, by regressing log $P/(1 - P)$ and time and using the estimated equation] is 57.3 percent.

In order to obtain the projections from equations 5.8 and 5.9, a set of assumptions must be made with respect to probable changes in prices of electricity and gas and in income. In any case, as argued earlier, equation 5.8 is not the right one to use; hence our projections will be only from equation 5.9.

Four cases will be considered for illustrative purposes. The resulting projections are given in Table 5.6. The projections are based on the assumption that the variables other than income and prices of electricity and gas will remain constant. These projections are generally higher than those obtained by straight trend-line projections. This is because of the strong income effect and the effect of natural gas prices shown by equation 5.9. Electric heating is actually in its early stages of growth compared with the use of other household electric appliances. Thus, it is possible that the next ten years will be the period corresponding to the middle portion of the logistic growth curve when the growth rate is faster, to be followed by a period of slower growth. Thus, projections of growth based on linear trend equations could actually underestimate the potential rate of growth during this period.

---

change causes only a movement along the demand curve. Therefore when relative prices of natural gas and electricity do not change (as shown going from situation A to situation B) we would expect a greater own-price effect from situation B resulting in a decrease in the percentage of electrically heated homes.

TABLE 5.6

Projections of the Proportion of Electrically
Heated Homes in 1985
(in percent)

	Rate of Growth of			
	Y	PE	PG	Estimate of P
Case 1	40.0	20.0	40.0	66.2
Case 2	40.0	20.0	20.0	60.7
Case 3	40.0	40.0	20.0	54.6
Case 4	20.0	20.0	20.0	57.1

Source: Compiled by the authors.

GROWTH IN ELECTRICALLY HEATED HOMES AND IN ELECTRICITY DEMAND

The previous analysis demonstrates that the proportion of electrically heated homes is sensitive to both price and income variables. Since the growth in electric heating is a major source of growth in electricity demand, it is worthwhile to examine how these two are related. For this purpose we estimated the demand equation

$$\ln Q = \alpha + \beta_1 \ln Q_{t-1} + \beta_2 \ln (PE) + \beta_3 \ln (RC)_t$$
$$+ \beta_4 \ln \left(\frac{HC}{RC}\right)_t + \beta_5 \ln (PCY) + \beta_6 \ln (PG)_t$$
$$+ \beta_7 \ln (HD + CD)_t \tag{5.10}$$

where Q   = quantity of electricity consumed
       PE   = average price of electricity
       RC   = number of residential electric customers
       HC   = number of customers with electric heating
       PCY = per capita income
       PG   = average price of gas
       HD   = number of heating degree days
       CD   = number of cooling degree days.

The equation was estimated from pooled cross-section and time-series data, using the cross-section and time dummies for the years 1962-72. The estimated equation was (with t-ratios in parentheses):

$$\ln Q = 0.392 + 0.296 \ln Q_{-1} - 0.415 \ln PE$$
$$(24.3) \phantom{\ln Q_{-1} - } (-16.5)$$

$$+ 0.706 \ln RC + 0.162 \ln \frac{HC}{RC} + 0.092 \ln PCY$$
$$ (42.6) (20.0) \phantom{\ln \frac{HC}{RC} + } (6.2)$$

$$+ 0.232 \ln PG + 0.091 \ln (HD + CD), \quad R^2 = 0.991.$$
$$ (3.8) (3.5)$$

It can be easily seen that the proportion of electrically heated homes is a very important explanatory variable. But the fact that the price and income variables are significant, even after inclusion of the proportion of electrically heated homes, suggests that these variables affect electricity demand both directly and indirectly through electric heating.

CONCLUSIONS

This chapter analyzes the determinants of the growth of electric heating in the TVA area, which has the highest percentage of electrically heated homes in the United States. Though the aggregate data show a smooth trend that is almost linear, the disaggregated data by distributors show marked differences, and it is shown that these differences at the disaggregated level are systematically related to per capita income, price of gas, price of electricity, gas availability, and weather variables. All these variables have been found to be highly important determinants of the growth in electric heating.

The report makes use of the logistic growth function and analyzes the detailed data available by distributors by first estimating the logistic functions. The results obtained are not as good as we expected initially, because in almost all cases the growth curve has not yet tapered off, and consequently we lack observations on the tail end of the logistic function. The methods we have employed are nevertheless potentially very useful and theoretically very appealing (see Bain[5] and Griliches[6]). Our analysis also points out some difficulties that other investigators using these methods are likely to encounter.

We have also estimated a pooled cross-section time series regression by using the linear probability model and a logit transform of the probabilities. Per capita income, prices of electricity and natural gas, gas availability index, and a weather index were used as explanatory variables. The linear probability model cannot be considered as giving good results in spite of the impressive R^2s and "correct" signs and significant estimates for all coefficients. However, the logit model gave very good results.

In conclusion, we made projections for the proportion of heating customers by 1985 from the linear trend equation, the logistic trend equation, and the logit equation with the explanatory variables mentioned earlier. The predictions made from the last two methods were higher than those made from straight trend extrapolation. Admittedly, the estimated logit equations are not entirely satisfactory, but our results point out that straight trend extrapolations may not be the correct model to use. Though it is often argued that the trend extrapolation methods overestimate demand as compared with those that take account of price and income variables, in this particular case the bias seems to be reversed.

NOTES

1. K. P. Anderson, "Residential Demand for Electricity: Econometric Estimates for California and the United States," Journal of Business (October 1973): 526-53.

2. National Economic Research Associates, unpublished paper (informal communication from Louis A. Guth, December 1974).

3. F. R. Oliver, "Methods of Estimating the Logistic Growth Function," Applied Statistics 13, no. 2 (1964): 57-66.

4. Z. Griliches, "Hybrid Corn: An Exploration in the Economics of Technological Change," Econometrica, October 1957.

5. A. D. Bain, "The Growth of Demand for New Commodities," Journal of the Royal Statistical Society, a Series, 1963.

6. Griliches, op. cit.

6

APPALACHIAN COAL:
SUPPLY AND DEMAND
William W. Lin

Several recent studies of the energy situation in the United States all point out that domestic coal supplies will likely play a key role in the nation's energy future. According to President Carter's energy plan, the utility industry will be asked to convert from gas and oil to coal over a period of time in generating electricity. This undoubtedly will add further demands for coal.

In 1900 about 212 million tons of bituminous coal were produced in the United States, almost none of this produced by strip mines. The negligible share of strip-mined coal in its early history was due largely to the lack of large mining equipment and machinery suitable for shipping overburden at that time. In the last decade, strip mining has significantly increased its share of total U.S. coal production as a result of improved mining technology and equipment. In 1970 the market share of strip-mined coal reached about 47 percent at the national level. With domestic coal demand expected to grow at a rate of 3.5 percent and exports at 4.5 percent a year from 1970 to 1985, the pressure to strip additional acreage will continue as strippable reserves are available.

Research sponsored by the National Science Foundation RANN Program under Union Carbide Corporation's contract with the U.S. Energy Research and Development Administration. Such support does not imply endorsement, agreement with, or official acceptance of the research results contained herein.

The region of Appalachia is defined as the geographic area in the Federal Coal Producing Districts 1, 2, 3, 4, 6, 7, and 13 as defined in the Bituminous Coal Act of 1937.

While this country has been striving for energy self-sufficiency, environmental degradation resulting from surface mining appears to be a vital environmental concern. Strip mining causes virtually complete destruction of the land surface. This adverse effect is particularly felt in Appalachia, for the coal found in the Appalachian Mountains was originally deposited in horizontal layers. The environmental impacts of strip mining are not confined to landscape alteration in the directly disturbed areas. Landslides, aesthetic erosion, and siltation are problems which continue for years after the completion of mining.

Nearly every state in which surface mines now operate has a reclamation law. Appalachia, an important coal region in which about 129 million tons of strip-mined bituminous coal were produced in 1972, is no exception. Nevertheless, state environmental laws vary from one state to another. In 1975, the Ford administration twice vetoed a strip-mining bill which would have required the coal miners to

1. Restore the affected land to its approximate original contour by backfilling, compacting (to ensure stability and to prevent leaking of toxic materials), and grading.
2. Prevent landslides and substantial erosion during mining and reclamation operations.
3. Fill all auger holes with an impervious and noncombustible material to prevent acid water drainage.
4. Minimize the disturbances to the prevailing hydrologic balance at the mine site and in associated offsite areas and to the quality and quantity of water in surface and groundwater systems.
5. Refrain from surface coal mining within 500 feet from active and abandoned underground mines in order to prevent breakthroughs and to protect health and safety of miners.
6. Ensure that the construction, maintenance, and postmining condition of access roads into and across the site of operation will control or prevent erosion and siltation, pollution of water, damage to fish or wildlife or their habitat, and damage to public or private property.
7. Refrain from the construction of roads or other access ways up a stream bed or drainage channel or in such proximity to such a channel so as to seriously alter the normal flow of water.
8. Establish a diverse, effective, and permanent vegetative cover native to the area of land to be affected and assume the responsibility for successful revegetation.

In addition, the proposed federal law would have banned coal strip mining in national forests and established that ranchers in the West, where the federal government owns the coal underneath the surface, could refuse to allow strip mining on their properties.

The rationale for President Ford's veto was reportedly based on estimates that the legislation would lead to the reduction of strip-mined coal production by anywhere from 40 to 126 million tons a year and cost 36,000 jobs, notably in the steep-slope mines of the Appalachian coal fields where joblessness is chronically high.

The purposes of this chapter are threefold: to develop a process analysis model capable of deriving short-run coal supply function under alternative requirements of land reclamation; to develop a short-run demand model for Appalachian coal; and to provide some empirical evidence of the short-run impacts of land reclamation on strip mining costs, delivered prices of coal, strip-mined coal production, and employment in Appalachia. In this chapter a process analysis model is developed which, in turn, is used to obtain cost estimates of surface mining and strip-mined coal supply functions in Appalachia under alternative requirements of land reclamation; short-run demand functions for Appalachia coal are developed and estimated; coal supply and demand curves are integrated to analyze the short-run impacts of land reclamation on coal price, strip-mined coal production, and regional employment in Appalachia.

COAL SUPPLY: A PROCESS ANALYSIS MODEL

The marginal cost curves for surface-mined coal (with and without reclamation) show a set of output-cost relations, each providing minimum selling prices for specified levels of coal production. Under the conditions of competitive market structure, the marginal cost curves are equivalent to industry supply curves when marginal cost exceeds minimum average variable cost. The purpose of this section is to develop a process analysis model which, in turn, is used to obtain cost estimates of surface mining and strip-mined coal supply functions in Appalachia under alternative requirements of land reclamation.

The concentration ratio in Appalachia is quite high. In 1970 the four largest coal companies accounted for 32.1 percent of the total coal production in Appalachia. Nevertheless, there is evidence that entry and exit to the industry is relatively easy. Therefore, market concentration is of some concern but not necessarily an indicator of deterioration in competitive structure or performance of the bituminous coal industry in Appalachia. Assuming a competitive structure, the coal supply curves were derived using the following process analysis model:

Minimize $Z = C'X$ subject to $A X \leq b$

where $b = (b_1, \ldots, b_i, \ldots, b_m)'$

$b_i = b_i^o \ (1 \pm \delta k)$

$Z =$ value of the objective function (total variable cost)

$C' =$ a $(1 \times n)$ row vector of unit variable costs

$X =$ a $(n \times 1)$ column vector of levels of the possible production processes, X_j, in terms of tonnage of coal extracted

$A =$ a $(m \times n)$ matrix including the following elements:
 (1) input-output coefficients denoting the amount of the ith constrained resources consumed per unit of process j;
 (2) coefficients (either -1 or 1) appearing in the material (interprocess) balance constraints;
 (3) coefficients appearing in the land reclamation constraint.

$b =$ a $(m \times 1)$ column vector of constraints including labor and equipment availabilities, a prespecified coal production level (b_i), right-hand sides of material balance constraints and land reclamation constraint, if appropriate

$b_i^o =$ the 1972 base-year strip-mined coal production

$\delta =$ a percentile increment in output for each corresponding observation along the cost curve

$k =$ a constant integer varying parametrically from zero to a maximum possible value at which the production of coal first becomes infeasible or simply irrelevant.

There are several distinguishing features of this model. First, production function of strip-mined coal is captured in the traditional linear programming or activities analysis framework. Second, linear constraints of the resource vector including mining machinery, equipment, and labor availabilities are incorporated into the constraint vector. Third, interprocess material balance constraints ensure that quantity of coal extracted in any stage of the strip-mining process has to be greater than or equal to the volume of coal extracted in the succeeding stage. Thus, for example, drilled coal obtained from drilling and shooting has to be greater than or equal to exposed coal obtained from overburden removal stage. Fourth, land reclamation constraint is incorporated to reflect various backfilling requirements in the mining process.

To reflect the regional differences in the characteristics of mining sites and coal deposits, and the prevailing prices of labor, equipment, and other inputs in the model, the coal-producing region of Appalachia is disaggregated into three homogeneous producing subregions: Northern Appalachia, Central Appalachia, and Southern Appalachia. Definitions of these regions, together with a statement of the physical parameters which describe the mining conditions in each region, are presented in Table 6.1.

TABLE 6.1

Description of Appalachian Subregions

Subregion	Production Parameters		
	Average Terrain Angle (degrees)	Seam Thickness (inches)	Maximum Overburden Height (feet)
1. Northern Appalachia (including Pa., Md., Ohio, and Districts 1, 3, 6 of northern W. Va.)	15	42	110
2. Central Appalachia (including Districts 7 and 8 in southern W. Va., Va., eastern Kentucky, and upper east Tenn.)	23	50	85
3. Southern Appalachia (including Alabama and District 13 in Tenn.)	15	30	90

Source: Compiled by the author.

The vector of production process (X), as is shown in activity columns of Table 6.2, starts with access-road construction and ends with auxiliary activities associated with the coal extraction process. Representative sets of activities were determined by reference to the technical literature,[1] Bureau of Mines data on actual equipment employed in each region,[2] and with the assistance of a mining engineering consultant firm.[3]

The matrix of technical coefficients (A) was calculated as follows:

$$a_{ij} = (S_t/R_{ij})/X_{jt},$$

TABLE 6.2

Initial Tableau of the Process Analysis Model for Northern Appalachia: 100 percent Backfill, 1972 Production Level

Constraints \ Activities	Access road construction	Scalping	Dozer/loader truck	Loader/truck	< 6 pan	6–15 pan	16–50 pan	Vertical drill	Horizontal drill
			Topsoil removal replacement					Drilling and shooting	
C_i	.00631	.00792	.09674	.07757	.21722	.10032	.02073	1.15317	1.07026
	X_1	X_2	X_3	X_4	X_5	X_6	X_7	X_8	X_9
1. Dozer	.00028	.00035	.00085						
2. Loader			.00170	.0017					
3. < 6 pan					.00850				
4. 6–15 pan						.00378			
5. 16–50 pan							.00092		
6. Vertical drill								.00976	
7. Horizontal drill									.00627
8. < 6 shovel									
9. 6–15 drag. or shovel									
10. 16–50 drag. or shovel									
11. > 50 dr. or shovel									
12. Auger									
13. 20-ton truck			.00170						
14. Off road truck				.00170					
15. Aux. equip.									
16. Sh/dr/lo operator									
17. Bull/pan operator	.00028	.00035	.00085		.00850	.00378	.00092		
18. Driller and shooter								.01952	.01254
19. Auger operator									
20. Truck driver			.00170	.00170					
21. Prodn support									
22. Maint. & repair								.01952	.01881
23. Ac. road coal	−1	+1							
24. Cleared coal		−1	+1	+1	+1	+1	+1		
25. Topsoil coal			−1	−1	−1	−1	−1		
26. Drilled coal								+1	+1
27. Exposed coal								−1	−1
28. Loaded & augered coal									
29. Hauled coal									
30. Auxed coal									
31. Final surface coal									
32. Vert. drilling								1.0	
33. Pan-use limit									
34. Backfilling									

2.94516	4.02057	3.18835	3.08961	2.32644	1.23187	4.76659	4.93952	8.21192	6.39815	7.23557	4.77147	1.27358
Overburden removal												
Transverse						Lateral						
Dozer	Loader	Dozer/ loader	6 -15 drag. or shovel	16–50 drag. or shovel	> 50 drag. or shovel	Loader/ truck	Dozer/ loader/ truck	6–15 d. or s/ truck	16–50 d. or s/ truck	< 6 pan	6–15 pan	16–50 pan
X_{10}	X_{11}	X_{12}	X_{13}	X_{14}	X_{15}	X_{16}	X_{17}	X_{18}	X_{19}	X_{20}	X_{21}	X_{22}
.13061		.05224	.03483	.02458	.00582		.05224	.05805	.04097	.52242	.23219	
	.20897	.10448				.10448	.05224					
										.52242		
											.23219	
												.05648
			06966					.11609				
				.02458					.04097			
					.00582							
						.10448	.10448	.11609	.08195			
	.20897	.10448	.06966	.02458	.00582	.10448	.05224	.11609	.04097			
.13061		.05224	.03483	.02458	.00582		.05224	.05805	.04097	.52242	.23219	.05648
						.10448	.10448	.11609	.16390			
			.06966	.02458	.00582			.11609	.04097			
+1	+1	+1	+1	+1	+1	+1	+1	+1	+1	+1	+1	+1
−1	−1	−1	−1	−1	−1	−1	−1	−1	−1	−1	−1	−1
−.25	−.25	−.25				−.25	−.25			−.25	−.25	−.25
										+1	+1	+1
11.88	11.88	11.88	11.88	11.88	11.88	−3.06	−3.06	−3.06	−3.06	−3.06	−3.06	−3.06

(continued)

(Table 6.2 continued)

		Backfill					Coal loading		Augering	Coal haulage	Revegetation	Auxiliary	B
		Dozer	Loader	6–15 drag or shovel	16–50 drag or shovel	>50 drag or shovel	Loader	>6 shovel					
		.03469	.07696	.13505	.10681	.05895	.04810	.03568	.72452	.25950	0	.17215	
		X_{23}	X_{24}	X_{25}	X_{26}	X_{27}	X_{28}	X_{29}	X_{30}	X_{31}	X_{32}	X_{33}	
		.00154	.00400	.00167	.00118	.00028	.00250						≤14,733,600
													≤7,803,600
													≤310,800
													≤268,800
													≤2,469,600
				.00333				.00317					≤705,600
													≤9,231,600
													≤2,772,000
													≤176,400
													≤42,000
													≤319,200
									.01613	.0250		.0325	≤84,000,000
													≤84,000,000
													≤84,000,000
		.00154	.00400	.00333	.00118	.00028	.00250	.00317	.01613	.0250			≤4,701,600
				.00167	.00118	.00028							≤3,583,200
						.00028							≤1,939,200
									.03230	.0250		.0052	≤319,200
												.0220	≤3,264,000
													≤5,728,800
													≤3,285,600
							+1	+1		+1	+1	+1	≤0
							−1	−1	−1	−1	−1	−1	≤0
													≤0
													≤0
													≤0
													≤0
													≤−170,555
													≤0
		−1	−1	−1	−1	−1							≤−70,876,000
							−.25	−.25					≤0
													≤0
													≤0

Source: Compiled by the author.

102

where a_{ij} = the input-output coefficient of constrained resource
                   i for activity j

S_t = the magnitude (in physical terms) of the task t to be
         performed, a function of mining conditions such as
         angle of the terrain, maximum highwall height, and
         so on

R_{ij} = the rate at which the ith input of process j performs
          task t, also a function of physical conditions at the
          mine

X_{jt} = output of process j in performing task t (tons of
          processed coal, a function of seam thickness).

Estimates of task sizes (S_t), as well as activity output (X_{jt}),
were based on cross-sectional diagrams of typical mine pits pos-
sessing the dimensions specified by the mine parameters, then extrapolated to encompass an assumed 1,000 linear feet of bench.
Machine and labor performance rates (R_{ij}) were estimated by the
engineering consultants[4] and reflect those mining conditions (principally terrain angle) which influence equipment performance.

The constraint vector (b) includes the limited availabilities of
equipment, labor inputs, interactivity balance constraints, surface
coal output, limitations on vertical drilling and pan-use, and backfilling requirement. Equipment availabilities were based on the
assumed maximum feasible availability (8,760 hr./year) of the
equipment reported by the Bureau of Mines to have been employed.
Labor availability was based on Bureau of Mines estimates of the
number of men working daily, allocated to occupation classes according to the Bureau of Labor Statistics 1967 Industry Wage Survey.[5] The maximum availability per worker was assumed to be
2,400 hr./year. Interactivity balance constraints are imposed to
ensure that the amount of coal processed in a given activity does
not exceed the amount of coal processed in the preceding activity.

The backfilling constraint, shown in the last row of Table 6.2,
is based on engineering considerations.
Let

γ = ratio of pit volume in bank cubic yards (BCY) to ton-
         nage of exposed coal

R = ratio of loose cubic yards (LCY) of overburden to ton-
     nage of exposed coal

α_t = fraction of transversely excavated spoil that automat-
          ically remains in the mine pit (= 0.25)

α_1 = fraction of laterally excavated spoil that is automat-
          ically backfilled (= 1.00)

f_w = desired or required pit-fill factor.

According to the activities in Table 6.2, then

$$f_w \leq (\alpha_i R(X_{10} + \cdots + X_{15}) + \alpha_1 R(X_{16} + \cdots + X_{22})$$
$$+ (X_{23} + \cdots + X_{27}))/\gamma(\sum_{j=10}^{22} X_j)$$

or

$$(\gamma f_w - \alpha_i R)(X_{10} + \cdots + X_{15}) + (\gamma f_w - \alpha_i R)(X_{16} + \cdots + X_{22})$$
$$- (X_{23} + \cdots + X_{27}) \leq 0$$

Based on a 1,000-foot mine section and the production parameters of Northern Appalachia in Table 6.1, it was calculated that

$$R = 995,930.62/49,987.89 = 19.9234$$
$$\gamma = 843,029.56/49,987.89 = 16.8647.$$

In the case of 100 percent backfill, then

$$\gamma f_w - \alpha_t R = 11.88$$
$$\gamma f_w - \alpha_1 R = -3.06.$$

In the vector of process costs (C), equipment operating costs were estimated by the engineering consultants and include fuel, lubricants, tires (if any), and repair parts. Labor wage rates by occupation were based on the 1967 Industrial Wage Survey inflated to 1972 conditions. Wage rates include average straight-time earnings, plus average overtime and shift-differential premiums. Materials and supplies were not identified as separate constrained inputs, but their costs are included in the process cost estimates.

Table 6.3 summarizes the results of the process analysis. The reader is cautioned that these results should be considered preliminary pending further validation. The marginal cost at each output level is taken to be the shadow price corresponding to the output constraint. As expected, the marginal costs increase stepwise according to the classical shape of marginal cost curves over the range of output conditions. In addition, a comparison of the average costs at different pit-fill factors* for a given output level provides

---

*The pit-fall factor refers to the extent to which the mine pit is backfilled with spoil material following coal extraction. Usually,

TABLE 6.3

Estimated Average and Marginal Costs of Coal Surface Mining in Appalachia, 1972

Production Level (1,000 tons)	Zero Backfill, $/Ton Average Cost	Marginal Cost	50% Backfill, $/Ton Average Cost	Marginal Cost	100% Backfill, $/Ton Average Cost	Marginal Cost
			Northern Appalachia			
56,701 (0.80)[a]	3.91	4.50	4.26	4.89	4.58	5.22
60,245 (0.35)	3.95	4.50	4.29	4.89	4.62	5.22
63,789 (0.90)	3.98	4.50	4.33	4.89	4.66	5.46
67,332 (0.95)	4.01	4.50	4.36	4.89	4.70	6.22
70,876 (1.00)	4.03	4.50	4.39	5.11	4.78	6.22
74,420 (1.05)	4.05	4.50	4.42	5.11	4.88	7.08
77,964 (1.10)	4.05	4.70	4.49	6.59	b	b
81,508 (1.15)	4.11	4.70	4.58	6.59	b	b
85,051 (1.20)	4.18	8.15	b	b	b	b
88,595 (1.25)	b	b	b	b	b	b
			Central Appalachia			
35,643 (0.80)	2.93	2.99	3.38	3.45	3.60	3.67
37,879 (0.85)	2.94	2.99	3.38	3.45	3.60	3.67
40,098 (0.90)	2.94	2.99	3.39	3.45	3.62	3.82
42,326 (0.95)	2.95	2.99	3.39	3.59	3.63	3.82
44,553 (1.00)	2.95	2.99	3.40	3.59	3.64	3.82
46,781 (1.05)	2.95	2.99	3.41	3.59	3.65	3.82
49,009 (1.00)	2.96	2.99	3.42	3.59	3.66	3.82
51,236 (1.15)	2.96	3.11	3.43	3.59	3.67	3.82
53,464 (1.20)	2.97	3.11	3.44	3.59	3.68	3.82
55,692 (1.25)	2.98	3.11	3.45	3.59	3.69	3.82
57,919 (1.30)	2.99	3.11	3.46	3.59	3.71	4.95
60,147 (1.35)	2.99	3.11	3.46	3.59	3.76	4.95
62,375 (1.40)	3.00	3.11	3.47	3.59	b	b
64,603 (1.45)	b	b	b	b	b	b
			Southern Appalachia			
11,043 (0.80)	3.94	4.84	4.45	5.38	4.82	5.90
11,734 (0.85)	3.99	4.84	4.51	5.53	4.88	5.90
12,424 (0.90)	4.04	4.84	4.57	5.53	4.95	7.01
13,114 (0.95)	4.09	4.98	4.62	5.53	5.06	7.02
13,804 (1.00)	4.13	4.98	4.67	5.53	5.16	7.02
14,494 (1.05)	4.17	4.98	4.72	5.77	b	b
15,185 (1.10)	4.21	4.98	4.79	7.49	b	b
15,875 (1.15)	4.25	5.19	b	b	b	b
16,565 (1.20)	4.29	5.19	b	b	b	b
17,255 (1.25)	4.41	9.13	b	b	b	b
17,945 (1.30)	b	b	b	b	b	b

[a]Figures in parentheses represent fractions of the 1972 production level.
[b]Infeasible with specified labor and equipment constraints.
Source: Compiled by the author.

approximate estimates of the cost of reclamation.* For example, the incremental cost of obtaining full rather than zero percent back-fill, while maintaining 1972 output, would have been $0.75/ton in Northern Appalachia.

Admittedly, mined land reclamation entails activities other than backfilling and grading the depleted mine pit and replacing the topsoil. Current reclamation practices, as required by KRS 350 in Kentucky, for example, include measures to enhance spoil bank stability and provide for improved water drainage characteristics. Prompt revegetation of disturbed land areas is also required to re-duce erosion. Because these measures tend to reduce the frequency of landslides and prevent the deterioration of water quality down-stream from the mine, they are properly a part of the reclamation process and their costs should be included in the total. However, an independent study has shown that backfilling, grading, and top-soil replacement constitute the principal components of the overall cost of reclamation. [6] For example, the study cited considers a model mine which is located on a slope of 20° and mined to a maxi-mum highwall height of 90 feet by conventional mining methods. An engineering cost analysis of this model mine shows that the total operating costs of full reclamation amount to $2.44/ton of coal mined, of which $2.26/ton is for backfilling and grading, $0.10/ton is for topsoil replacement, and $0.08/ton is for revegatation. Taken together, backfilling, grading, and topsoil replacement account for 93 percent of the total operating costs of full reclamation and may, therefore, be used as a proxy variable for overall reclamation costs.

APPALACHIAN COAL DEMAND ESTIMATION

The requirement of a given level of land reclamation tends to limit coal production potential; however, the impact cannot be fully assessed without knowing the structural relationship of coal demand. This is so because supply and demand determine the market price, which, in turn, determines the quantity of coal ultimately produced and consumed.

As is shown in Table 6.4, the five major uses for Appalachian coal are as boiler fuel for generating electricity (steam coal), as a raw material for making coke (coking coal), as fuel in the production

---

but not always, the greater the pit-fill factor, the higher the level of reclamation obtained.

*Includes topsoil replacement and backfilling and excludes revegetation.

of a variety of industrial products (industrial coal), domestic export, and overseas export. In this chapter the first four coal demand equations were estimated separately by the use of ordinary least squares. Overseas export demand was not estimated since it is more likely to be influenced by the economic conditions of the importing countries (mainly Japan and Canada) and worldwide coal production than by the delivered price of coal in Appalachia. Retail coal demand was also not estimated for two reasons: its quantity is negligible, and the retail demand is based principally on nonprice factors, such as the cleanliness and convenience of competing fuels.[7]

TABLE 6.4

Consumption of Appalachian Bituminous Coal, 1972

Consumer Class	Consumption and Exports (millions of tons)	Percent
Steam-electric utility industry	152.7	41
Coke industry	50.4	13
General industry	30.7	8
Exports		
Domestic	81.6	22
Oversea	55.9	15
Retail deliveries	3.2	1
Total	374.5	

Source: Compiled from the U.S. Bureau of Mines Mineral Yearbook, 1972.

Since coal is primarily used for steam electric generation, for making coke, and for the production of a variety of industrial products, coal demands are derived demands. According to the theory of derived demand, demand for an input is a function of factor prices (for example, labor and capital) and the product price. The coal demand equations are thus generally specified as functions of the delivered prices of coal, prices of substitute inputs, outputs, and time trends. In mathematical expression, the coal demand equations were specified in the following log-linear form:

$$\ln Q_{ct} = \alpha + \beta \ln Z_t + \mu t$$

where l   = the time period
       Q_c = quantity of coal consumed
       Z^c = a vector of explanatory variables
       μ_t = the error term.

Most strip-mined coal is consumed by the electric utility industry. Virtually no strip-mined coal is metallurgical coal--a coal market that demands high-quality coal and thus is dominated by underground coal. In this instance, surface-mined coal is rarely a real substitute for underground coal. Accordingly, it would be desirable to focus this study upon spot and contract markets for steam coal. The unavailability of detailed statistical data on steam coal consumption by mining source and by state for years prior to 1973, however, makes this approach extremely difficult, if not impossible. In addition, the fact that about 50 percent of the steam coal consumed in 1973 in Appalachia comes from underground coal further compounds this difficulty. One way to take this into account is to assume a fixed proportion of market share for strip-mined coal in this market. However, this assumption is unjustifiable because a shift in market share would undoubtedly occur if full reclamation were required. Therefore, in this study the individual coal demands are simply synthesized into an aggregated coal demand curve.

Direct data on regional coal consumption according to consumer use are not listed in the Bureau of Mines Mineral Yearbook (volume of fuels). However, the Mineral Yearbook does provide information on the volume of coal distributed to each consuming state and by consumer use. It was found that distribution data alone cannot accurately approximate consumption data and that failure to make this adjustment yields incorrect signs for some important variables. Therefore, coal consumption data were derived indirectly by incorporating the annual net stock change according to consumer uses into the distribution data for the region. Regional data are used when possible. In the cases of wage rates, Federal Reserve Board Index of industrial production, and industrial coal prices, national data were used because regional data are currently lacking. All price variables are deflated by the wholesale price index of intermediate material.

The results of the regression analysis for the period from 1957 to 1973 and the definitions of variables are presented in Tables 6.5 and 6.6. As expected, oil and natural gas are found to be substitutes for coal in electric generation, although steam coal demand seems to be highly price inelastic in the short run. Contrary to Reddy's empirical finding,[8] the price of natural gas for steam electric generation not only shows a correct positive sign, but is also statistically

TABLE 6.5

Estimated Demand Equations for Appalachian Coal, 1957-73[*]

---

1. Steam coal

$$\ln Q_{sc} = -1.258^\dagger - 0.165\ \ln P^\dagger_{sc} + 0.216\ \ln P^\ddagger_{oa} + 0.144\ \ln P^\ddagger_{sg} + 0.899\ \ln E^\dagger_{a}$$

$$(0.316)\ (0.073) \qquad\qquad (0.091) \qquad\qquad (0.081) \qquad\qquad (0.022)$$

$$R^2 = 0.997 \quad d = 1.75^{***}$$

2. Coking coal

$$\ln Q_{cc} = 2.232^\ddagger - 0.482\ \ln P^{**}_{cc} + 0.653\ \ln I^\dagger + 0.620\ \ln W^\dagger - 0.181\ \ln T^\ddagger$$

$$(0.932)\ (0.351) \qquad\qquad (0.141) \qquad\quad (0.403) \qquad\quad (0.068)$$

$$R^2 = 0.822 \quad d = 2.45^{***}$$

3. Industrial coal

$$\ln Q_{ic} = 0.504 - 0.819\ \ln P^\dagger_{ic} + 0.822\ \ln P^{**}_{ig} + 0.307\ \ln F^{**} - 0.126\ \ln T^\ddagger$$

$$(2.410)\ (0.154) \qquad\qquad (0.495) \qquad\quad (0.201) \qquad\quad (0.068)$$

$$R^2 = 0.724 \quad d = 2.04^{***}$$

4. Domestic export

$$\ln Q_{de} = 6.298^\dagger - 1.322\ \ln P^\dagger_{sc} + 0.124\ \ln P^{**}_{oi} + 0.373\ \ln E^\dagger_{i} - 0.116\ \ln T^\dagger$$

$$(0.461)\ (0.075) \qquad\qquad (0.092) \qquad\quad (0.069) \qquad\quad (0.028)$$

$$R^2 = 0.967 \quad d = 2.11^{***}$$

---

[*]Figures in parentheses are estimated standard errors; R is the co-correlation between the observed and estimated values of the dependent variable; d is the Durbin-Watson statistic.

[†]Statistically significant at 1 percent level.

[‡]Statistically significant at 10 percent level.

[**]Statistically significant at 20 percent level.

[***]No serial correlation in the residuals.

Source: Compiled by the author.

TABLE 6.6
Definition of Variables and Sources of Data

Variable	Definition	Unit of Measurement	Source of Data
Q_{sc}	Consumption of Appalachian steam coal by the electric utility industry	Millions of tons	1
P_{sc}	Average delivered price of steam coal in Appalachia, weighted by steam-electric generation by utility industry in each state of the region	Cents/million Btu	2
P_{oa}	Average cost of oil for electric generation in Appalachia, weighted by consumption of oil in electric utility industry in each of the states	Cents/million Btu	2
P_{sg}	Average cost of natural gas for electric generation, weighted by consumption of natural gas in electric utility industry in each of the states	Cents/million Btu	2
E_a	Steam-electric generation in Appalachia	Billions of kwh	2
Q_{cc}	Consumption of Appalachian coking coal	Millions of tons	1
P_{cc}	Average cost of coking coal at merchant coke ovens weighted by coal carbonized in each of the states	Dollars/ton	1
I	Pig Iron production in Appalachia	Millions of tons	8
T	Time trend variable (1957 = 1, 1958 = 2, etc.)		
Q_{ic}	Consumption of Appalachian industrial coal by general industry	Millions of tons	1
P_{ic}	Delivered price of industrial coal in the United States	Dollars/ton	3
P_{ig}	Average industrial price of natural gas, weighted by the volume of natural gas consumed by general industry in each state of the region	Cents/million cubic feet	1
F	Federal Reserve Board index of industrial production	1967 = 100 (mfg. industry only)	4,6
Q_{de}	Quantity of coal shipped from Appalachia to other domestic regions	Millions of tons	2
P_{oi}	Average cost of oil for steam-electric generation in the domestic importing region, weighted by coal shipment from Appalachia to each region	Cents per million Btu	2
E_i	Steam-electric generation in the domestic importing region	Billions of kwh	2
RFR	Railroad freight rate in the United States	Dollars per ton	5
W	Wage rate for industrial workers	Dollars per hour	6
WPI	Wholesale price index of intermediate material	1967 = 100	6,7

Sources of data:

1. U.S. Bureau of Mines, Mineral Yearbook (Volume of Fuels), 1957-73.

2. Edison Electric Institute, "Statistical Yearbook of the Electric Utility Industry" (New York, 1957-73).

3. Nallapu N. Reddy, The demand for coal in the United States: An econometric analysis, Proceedings of the American Institute of Mining, Metallurgical, and Petroleum Engineers, Inc. (AIME) Annual Meeting, Dallas, Texas, February 23-28, 1974.

4. Board of Governors of the Federal Reserve System, "Industrial Production: 1971 Edition" (Washington, D.C., November 1972).

5. National Coal Association, "Bituminous Coal Data, 1973 Edition," May 1974.

6. U.S. Department of Commerce, "Survey of Current Business," selected issues.

7. U.S. Department of Commerce, "Bituminous Statistics: The 17th Biennial Edition," a supplement to the Survey of Current Business, 1969.

8. U.S. Bureau of Mines, Mineral Yearbook (Volume of Metals), 1957-73.

significant. From an engineering standpoint, in the short run there is an almost fixed ratio between a unit of electricity generated and the amount of coal consumed. This suggests that labor may not be a real substitute for coal in generating electricity. Accordingly, wage rate was excluded as a variable in the steam coal demand equations.

Bituminous coal appears to be the primary fuel source for making coke, which, in turn, is used for making pig iron and steel. Hence, there are no price variables of substitutes appearing in the coking coal demand structural equation. The negative coefficient of time-trend variables implies less coal has been consumed per ton of pig iron. In fact, coking coal used per ton of pig iron has declined steadily from 2,200 pounds in 1960 to 1,800 pounds in 1972.

The primary users of industrial coal include steel and rolling mills, the portland cement industry, ceramic plants, chemicals and allied products, paper and allied products, and a host of other manufacturing industries. Since the Federal Reserve Board Index of industrial production is considered to be an appropriate indicator of demand for manufacturing products, it is used as the output variable.

As is shown in Table 6.4, the region of Appalachia exported about 22 percent of its coal production to the domestic importing regions in 1972, primarily to the Middle Atlantic, East North Central, South Atlantic, and Middle South Central Census regions. In theory, the volume of trade is determined by the price differential between the exporting region and importing region, assuming a constant transport cost. Here, the price differential was simplified by using the delivered price of coal in Appalachia as a proxy. The domestic export demand was found to be price elastic. This is because coal exported to other regions could be used as steam coal, coking coal, industrial coal, or even retail deliveries. The larger number of uses to which coal can be put in the importing regions would lead us to expect that the domestic export demand is more price elastic.

IMPACTS OF RECLAMATION ON COAL PRICE, PRODUCTION, AND EMPLOYMENT

As stated before, it is necessary to integrate coal supply and demand together in a market equilibrium framework before the impacts of land reclamation on coal price, coal production, and employment can be fully ascertained.

On the demand side, this means the demand for each submarket first must be combined into an aggregate coal demand, which is the horizontal summation of demand schedules for steam coal $(D_s D_s)$, coking coal $(D_c D_c)$, industrial coal $(D_i D_i)$, domestic export $(D_e D_e)$, oversea export, and retail deliveries, as shown in Figure 6.1.

FIGURE 6.1

Bituminous Coal Production in Appalachia
(millions of tons)

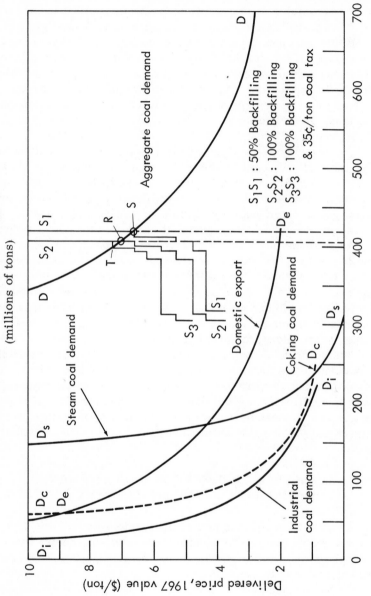

Source: Compiled from Bureau of Mines Data.

112

The individual demand schedules were derived separately by substituting proper values of the explanatory variables (except delivered prices of coal) in 1972 into the demand equations estimated from the regression analysis.

On the supply side, three adjustments must be made to maintain consistency with our demand estimation. First, the FOB minimum selling prices at each output level as obtained from the process analysis were converted into the equivalent delivered prices. The discrepancy between the average delivered price and FOB price of coal in Appalachia in 1972 was estimated as $0.70/ton,[9] mainly due to transportation cost and royalty. Second, the 1972 delivered price level was deflated by the wholesale price index of intermediate material. This is necessary because deflated prices were used throughout in the demand equations estimation. Third, the strip-mined coal supply is combined with an assumed perfectly inelastic underground and auger coal supply curve. The fact that underground mined coal production has remained fairly constant while coal prices varied suggests that the above assumption may not be unreasonable.

The step supply curves, with full reclamation (100 percent backfilling) and with current typical land reclamation practice (50 percent backfilling), are shown as S_2S_2, and S_1S_1, respectively, in Figure 6.1. As expected, the supply curve shifts upward and to the left when full reclamation is required. The vertical (inelastic) portion of the supply curves reflect the infeasibility of expanding production given the short-run constraints on the availabilities of inputs. In the context of comparative-static analysis, the resulting strip-mined coal production is expected to be reduced; however, the new market equilibrium price at point R is higher than the equilibrium price at point S by about $0.40/ton. Therefore, the higher market equilibrium price at point R induces an expansion of output which offsets a portion of the reduction in strip-mined coal production which otherwise would occur. A reduction of about 10 million tons of strip-mined coal production in Appalachia would have occurred in 1972 as a result of changing reclamation requirements from current typical reclamation practice to full reclamation. This represents about 8 percent of the actual 1972 strip-mining production of bituminous coal or 3 percent of the total coal production in Appalachia.

The effect in 1975 is probably much different. Given the major price rises for oil and natural gas, the above rather minimal impact would also tend to be temporary in nature. This seems likely to be the case since the continued effect of higher prices for oil and natural gas, coupled with governmental pressures, will lead to a substantial outward shift in the demand function for coal to be used in electric power generation. The result of that shift will probably vastly override any tendency toward a reduction in the quantity of coal produced and consumed due to the expense of reclamation activities.

The proposed strip-mining regulation requiring restoration of land to approximately its original contour is aimed at preventing further land deterioration in the future. How about lands scarred by the strip mining in the past? The congressional proposal to levy a 35¢/ton surface coal tax on future surface coal production to help pay for restoring the destroyed lands amounts to adding 35¢/ton to the marginal cost previously obtained for the case of 100 percent backfilling in the process analysis. The resulting supply curve, S_3S_3 in Figure 6.1 intersects with the aggregate coal demand curve DD at point T, indicating a further reduction of about 6 million tons of strip-mined coal would occur.

The direct short-run effect on employment in Appalachia resulting from legislation requiring full reclamation of strip-mined lands can be estimated once the short-run impact on coal production is known. First, the reduction in labor requirements, in terms of labor man-days, is calculated by dividing the 10 million tons by the average labor productivity at strip mines in Appalachia, 30.44 tons/ man-day. The total number of employees affected is then obtained by dividing this result by the average annual number of working days for strip mines in the region.

Our results show that imposing full reclamation requirements would have resulted in the loss of some 1,467 jobs for coal production workers in Appalachia in 1972. However, it should be noted that a portion of this estimated job loss would have been offset by the enhanced opportunities for employment arising from the expanded reclamation activities. In fact, it was found that about 582 employment opportunities would have been created as a result of the expanded reclamation activities, as are shown in Table 6.7. This estimation was based on the results of our process analysis, in which labor hours employed for each activity are shown in the optimal solution. According to the market equilibrium points R and S, as shown in Figure 6.1, we can thus easily identify the output levels and labor man-hours employed for reclamation activities. Hence, the additional reclamation requirement would have caused only a moderate net direct impact on employment, costing 885 employment opportunities or about 3 percent of the labor supply in the Appalachian strip-mining industry.

Of course, the severity of short-run impacts on coal production and employment can be mitigated if the law provides for an extended period before compliance or a gradual transition to the new reclamation requirements. Furthermore, these impacts tend to be temporary in nature. Given today's demand conditions over a longer period of time, the demand curves would be shifted outward to the right. On the other hand, the effect of the employment multiplier would increase the severity of short-run unemployment. Assuming a national employment multiplier of 1.80 for the coal industry,[10] our preliminary evaluation shows an overall job loss of no more than 1,593 production workers in Appalachia for the year 1972.

TABLE 6.7

Employment Opportunities Created by Reclamation
Activities in Appalachian Coal Mining Industry

	Subregion		
	Northern Appalachia	Central Appalachia	Southern Appalachia
Man-hours employed for reclamation			
50 percent backfill	326,362	249,871	91,797
100 percent backfill	1,100,449	706,251	258,549
Difference	774,087	456,380	166,752
Employment opportunity created by the additional reclamation activities*	323	190	69

*It is assumed, as was employed in the process analysis, that one man-year is equal to 2,400 man-hours; total equals 582.
Source: Compiled by the author.

CONCLUSIONS

This study provides, in quantitative terms, a preliminary evaluation of the impact of land reclamation on coal production costs, delivered prices, strip-mined coal production levels, and regional employment in the Appalachian coal industry. Our results show that full reclamation has rather minor impacts on the coal industry in Appalachia.

In 1972 the imposition of requirements for full rather than 50 percent reclamation of strip-mine-disturbed lands would have resulted in an increase of $0.35/ton in average coal production costs, the loss of about 10 million tons of strip-mine coal production in Appalachia, and an increase of about $0.40/ton in the delivered price of coal. In the short run, a further reduction of about 6 million tons of strip-mined coal would occur as a result of the induced change in coal supply arising from the proposed surface coal tax to help pay for the restoration of lands disturbed by strip mining in the past. The short-run, direct impact of full reclamation on employment is the loss of 885 jobs for production workers in the Appalachian coal-mining industry. The overall impact is the loss of no more than 1,593 jobs in Appalachia. (These effects would probably be greatly different in 1975 because of the major price rises which have occurred for oil and natural gas.) In any case, it is expected that the economic dislocations would tend to be temporary in nature.

TABLE 6.8

Estimated Economic Impacts of Proposed
Regulation of Coal Surface Mining

Source	Impacted Area	Jobs Lost	Coal Production Loss (millions of tons)
Administration estimates	United States	36,000	40 to 126
This study	Appalachia	1,593	10

Source: Compiled by the author.

It is recognized that these findings diverge sharply from estimates prepared elsewhere which were reportedly used as the rationale for the president's veto of the Federal Surface Mining Bill. However, the results described here are consistent with those obtained in other studies.[11] Table 6.8 highlights the most important differences between our findings and administration estimates. Since we do not know the basis of the administration estimates, we are unable to explain the large discrepancy between the findings of the two studies. Although different impacted areas are considered (United States versus Appalachia), this alone is insufficient to account for the observed differences in the findings. In 1972 Appalachia produced 47 percent of the total U.S. strip-mined bituminous coal. Using this proportional basis to expand the impacted area to include the United States as a whole still yields estimates of economic impacts which are dramatically lower than those of the administration.

NOTES

1. Mathematica, Inc. and Ford, Bacon and Davis, Inc., "Design of Surface Mining Systems in the Eastern Kentucky Coal Fields," Vol. 2, Report ARC-71-66-T1 (Washington, D.C.: Appalachian Regional Commission, 1974).

2. U.S. Bureau of Mines, Minerals Yearbook, 1957-73, Volume of Mineral Fuels (Washington, D.C.: U.S. Government Printing Office, 1958-74).

3. Gwin, Dobson and Foreman, Inc., "Final Report for the Oak Ridge National Laboratory on Strip Mining and Reclamation Methods in the Coal Industry in Appalachia" (Oak Ridge, Tenn.: Oak Ridge National Laboratory, 1974).

4. Ibid.

5. U.S. Bureau of Labor Statistics, "Industry Wage Survey: Bituminous Coal Mining," Bulletin No. 1583 (Washington, D.C., February 1968).

6. National Coal Association, "Highlights of a Busy Year for Coal," Coal Age 79 (February 1974): 70-71.

7. See Reed Moyer, Competition in the Midwestern Coal Industry (Cambridge, Mass.: Harvard University Press, 1964).

8. Nallapu N. Reddy, "The Demand for Coal in the United States: An Econometric Analysis," Proceedings of the American Institute of Mining, Metallurgical and Petroleum Engineers (AIME) Annual Meetings, Dallas, February 23-28, 1974.

9. See U.S. Bureau of Mines, Minerals Yearbook, 1972.

10. Telephone communication from William H. Miernyk, Regional Research Institute, West Virginia University, Morgantown.

11. Morris Goldstein and Robert S. Smith, "Land Reclamation Requirements and Their Estimated Effects on the Coal Industry," Journal of Environmental Economic Management 2 (1975): 135-49.

7

ESTIMATION OF
OPTIMAL INVENTORY OF
COAL STOCKS HELD
BY ELECTRIC UTILITIES
R. Blaine Roberts

Of prime importance in the national response to the energy crisis is the development of accurate forecasting models on a disaggregated (state or regional) basis. Particularly for short-term quarterly forecasting models, many real problems must be dealt with explicitly and rigorously that can often be ignored or finessed by more aggregate models or long-term models.

For example, at first blush it may seem that deliveries of coal to electric utilities would be closely related to consumption of coal in the quarter with some seasonality, because of weather and some allowance for deviations around strike periods. Since deliveries, by definition, are equal to consumption plus the change in stocks held by utilities, this amounts to saying that stocks fluctuate only because of seasonality and strikes.

Figure 7.1 illustrates that, for some states, there is a considerable seasonal variation in stocks. However, Figures 7.2 and 7.3 show that for many of the large electric-utility coal-using states, there is little evidence of seasonality.

Furthermore, there is no obvious pattern around the major strike periods of 1968:4, 1971:4, and 1974:4. Something more must be influencing those movements in stocks.

The author would like to acknowledge the helpful comments of G. S. Maddala, David Toof, and Myron Olstein. Financial support for a portion of this research was graciously provided by National Science Foundation Grant SOC-76-04356 to the University of Florida. Earlier research was partially supported by the Federal Energy Agency through a contract with Arthur Young & Company.

FIGURE 7.1

Average Quarterly Stock of Coal Held by Electric Utilities
in Michigan, 1967:1 to 1975:3
(millions of tons)

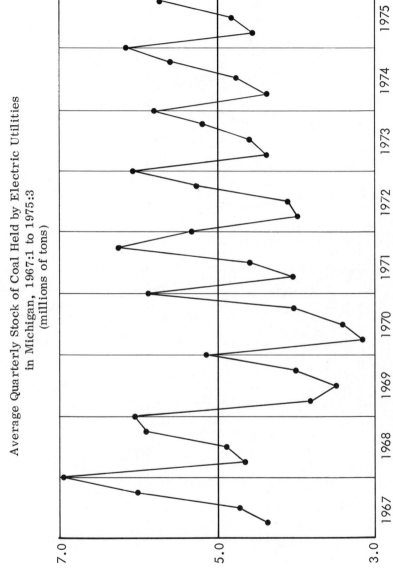

Source: Compiled by the author.

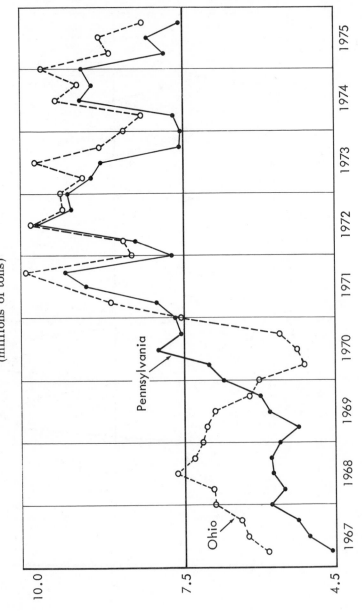

FIGURE 7.2

Average Quarterly Stock of Coal Held by Electric Utilities
in Pennsylvania and Ohio, 1967:1 to 1975:3

(millions of tons)

Pennsylvania

Ohio

Source: Compiled by the author.

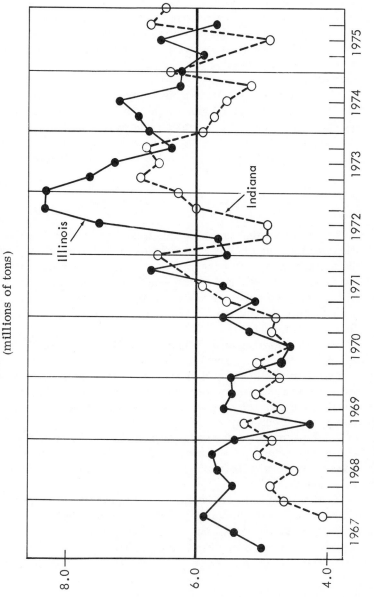

FIGURE 7.3

Average Quarterly Stock of Coal Held by Electric Utilities
in Illinois and Indiana, 1967:1 to 1975:3
(millions of tons)

Source: Compiled by the author.

121

To confirm the observation that changes in stocks by state are influenced by more than seasonality and strike expectations, preliminary regressions were run using a naive model. Deliveries were assumed to be a function of consumption with seasonal dummies and periods around strikes first omitted and, then, ad hoc strike dummies added. The results produced a standard error as percent of the mean of approximately 25 percent and, in some cases, even more. For a forecasting model, this size of error is generally unacceptable.

The following sections present the theoretical basis of the model, several practical alterations that were necessary to obtain the final equations to be estimated the techniques and data for estimation, and a summary of the empirical results for forecasting the stocks of coal held by electric utilities on a state-by-state basis.

THEORETICAL FRAMEWORK

Many changing forces and policies have affected electric utilities and their use of coal: the Clean Air Act, the oil embargo and the fourfold increase in petroleum prices, the introduction of stack scrubbers, the proposed forced-conversion programs, the introduction of and problems with nuclear generation capacity, shortages and proposed deregulation of natural gas, and several other energy conservation programs.

With regard to coal deliveries, utilities may jointly or wholly own coal mines; have short-, intermediate-, or long-term contracts with particular mines; own or subsidize the rolling stock to deliver the coal; or a number of other arrangements.[1] In addition, electric utilities are generally regulated and are required by law to meet the demand for electricity.

The literature on regulation of utilities has dealt only generally with factor inputs. The classic article is by Averch and Johnson.[2] More recent examples that incorporate uncertainty are Meyer[3] and Peles and Stein.[4]

Thus, the analysis begins by assuming that utilities attempt to minimize the cost of obtaining coal in an uncertain world subject to a minimum stock constraint. The determination of the stock constraint is discussed in more detail below.

The cost of coal purchases at any time is stated in equation 7.1:

$$M_t = P_t B_t + m(S_t) + b_1 SQ1B_t W_t + b_2 SQ2B_t W_t \qquad (7.1)$$

$$+ b_3 SQ3B_t W_t + b_4 SQ4B_t W_t$$

where M_t is cost at time t

P_t is price of coal at t

B_t is deliveries of coal at time t

$m(S_t)$ is the cost of holding an inventory of size S at t, given unit labor costs of W_t

S_t is the stock of coal at time t

SQ1 is seasonal dummy variable with a value of 1 in the first quarter and 0 for the second, third, and fourth quarters of each year

SQ2, SQ3, and SQ4 are similar seasonal dummies for the second, third, and fourth quarters, respectively

b_1, b_2, b_3, and b_4 are the real costs in terms of man-hours of delivering and handling a ton of coal in the first, second, third, and fourth quarters, respectively

W_t is an index of wage rates at time t.

The price of coal in the future is uncertain, but it is distributed around some expected price that depends upon economic conditions that affect the aggregate supply and demand for coal, as given in equation 7.2.

$$P_t = P(Y_t, U) \qquad\qquad (7.2)$$

where Y_t is a vector of known economic indicators of aggregate coal supply and demand

U is a random element with an expected value of zero and finite variance.

Thus, the expected future price is

$$E(P_t) = P(Y_t, O)$$

Since electric utilities are required to produce to meet the demand and for other reasons, one would expect utilities to be risk-averse. Thus, the decision to hold inventories can be characterized as the minimization of expected utility of cost as given in equation 7.3.

$$\text{Min } E[U(M)] \qquad\qquad (7.3)$$

Subject to $S_t \geq \overline{S}_t$ for all t

where $\overline{S}_t$ is a minimum stock that must be held at time t;

$$M = \sum_{t=0}^{\infty} \frac{M_t}{1 + r_t}$$

r_t is the compound rate of interest from the present to time t
$U'(m) < 0$, $U''(M) < 0$ for risk-averse utilities.

The first-order conditions for equation 7.3 to be a minimum are:

$$E[U'\left(\frac{P_t}{1+r_t} + \frac{m'(S_t)}{1+r_t} + \left(\sum_{i=1}^{4} b_i SQ_i\right) \frac{W_t}{1+r_t} + \frac{m'(S_{t+1})}{1+r_{t+1}}\right. \tag{7.4}$$

$$\left. + \ldots \right)] + \sum_{i=0}^{\infty} \lambda_{t+i} = 0$$

where λ_{t+i} is the Lagrangean multiplier for the minimum stock
constraint.

The first-order conditions will be sufficient if marginal storage cost is increasing. Equation 7.4 requires, in turn, that between
any two successive time periods:

$$E\left(\frac{P_{t+1}}{1+r_{t+1}}\right) - E\left(\frac{P_t}{1+r_t}\right) + \left(\sum_{i=1}^{4} b_{i+1} SQ_{i+1}\right) \frac{W_{t+1}}{1+r_{t+1}} \tag{7.5}$$

$$- \left(\sum_{i=1}^{4} b_i SQ_i\right) \frac{W_t}{1+r_t} + \frac{\text{cov}(U', P_{t+1}/(1+r_{t+1}))}{E(U')}$$

$$- \frac{\text{cov}(U', P_t/(1+r_t))}{E(U')} - \frac{\lambda_t}{E(U')(1+r_t)} = \frac{m'_t}{1+r_t}$$

where $SQ_5 = SQ_1$.

In the current period, the price of coal is known with certainty. Thus, for one period into the future, letting the current
period be denoted by t and if the minimum stock constraint is not
binding, equation 7.5 becomes:

$$(6) \quad \frac{E(P_{t+1})}{1+r_{t,t+1}} - P_t + \left(\sum_{i=1}^{4} b_{i+1} SQ_{i+1}\right) \frac{W_{t+1}}{1+r_{t,t+1}} \tag{7.6}$$

$$- \left(\sum_{i=1}^{4} b_i SQ_i\right) W_t + \frac{\text{cov}(U', P_{t+1})}{E(U')(1+r_{t,t+1})} = m'(S_t)$$

where $1+r_{t,t+1} = \dfrac{1+r_{t+1}}{1+r_t}$

If the utilities were risk-neutral, then the covariance term in equation 7.6 would be zero and 7.6 would state that the expected marginal gain from holding inventories (the difference between the future effective price of coal discounted by the interest cost of holding coal and the current effective price of coal plus the difference in delivery and handling costs) should be equal to the marginal cost of holding inventories when the minimum stock constraint is not effective. The covariance term in equation 7.6 represents the effect of risk aversion. For the risk-averse firm, cov $(U', P_{t+1}/1+r_{t,t+1})/E(U')$ is positive, and the risk-averse utility will hold an inventory such that the expected marginal gains are less than the marginal costs.

An interesting issue is how equation 7.6 can be made operational. In particular, how can the covariance term be measured? What a priori general form should be specified for the marginal cost function on the right-hand side of equation 7.6 ?

The immediate candidate as a proxy for uncertainty is the rate of change in the price of coal. The faster prices are rising or falling the more likely it is that uncertainty is higher. However, the percentage change in price is already approximated by the first two terms in equation 7.6. The next candidate is the level of coal prices. The hypothesis would have to be that the higher the price of coal, the more uncertainty there is likely to be about obtaining new supplies, continued deliveries, and so forth. Alternatively, it is not clear that a long period of sustained higher prices of coal would not have associated varying degrees of uncertainty. This opens the door for a large number of possible functional formulations of current and/or lagged values of the price of coal, perhaps relative to other fuel prices or to other prices in general.

As a first approximation, therefore, the covariance term in 7.6 is assumed to be a function of the future price of coal. Letting PX_t be the expected price differential; H_t, the seasonal handling cost differential; and $m'(S_t)$ the marginal costs of holding inventories, then 7.6 becomes:

$$PX_t + f\ (\frac{P_{t+1}}{1+r_{t,t+1}}) + H_t = m'\ (S_t) \qquad (7.7)$$

This relation is illustrated in Figure 7.4. S'_t is optimal for a risk-neutral firm and S_t^* is optimal for a risk-averse firm. For sufficiently low values of $PX_t + f(P_{t+1}/1+r_{t,t+1}) + H_t$, the firm would hold minimal inventories of $\bar{S}_t$. In this case, the Lagrangean multiplier term, $-\lambda_t/E(U')\ (1+r_{t,t+1})$, would be positive and have a value equal to the difference between $PX_t + f(P_{t+1}/1+r_{t,t+1}) + H_t$ and the marginal cost for $\bar{S}_t$.

FIGURE 7.4

Illustration of Optimal Inventory

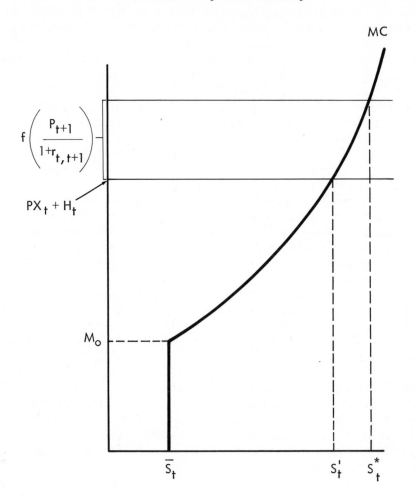

*S_t^* is the optimal stock for marginal costs given by MC, a risk-averse firm. S'_t is the optimal stock for a risk-neutral firm.

Source: Compiled by the author.

With regard to the minimal stock, $\overline{S}_t$, there are two problems: What determines the minimal stock? How can it be observed empirically? Clearly the minimal stock is nonnegative and it is not likely to be a constant over time. Furthermore, the minimal stock that utilities feel they must hold probably depends upon the degree of reliance on coal as the fuel for electrical generation. Therefore, $\overline{S}_t$ is taken to be a constant multiple of future consumption of coal or

$$\overline{S}_t = k_1 C_{t+1} \tag{7.8}$$

The question of how to estimate k_1 is taken up below.

The next issue is the functional form of the marginal cost function. Marginal costs must be positive and probably increase with the level of the stock. In addition, changes in capacity over time and changing factor costs must be considered. Given that there is a hypothesized minimal stock $\overline{S}_t = k_1 C_{t+1}$, costs to maintain the minimal stock must be considered as sunk or fixed costs. One of the simplest functional forms that satisfies these observations is shown in equation 7.9.

$$m'(S_t) = [m_0 + m_1 (S_t^* - k_1 C_{t+1})] W_t \tag{7.9}$$

where S_t^* is the desired, optimal stock at time t

k_1 is a constant multiple of future consumption of coal, C_{t+1}

m_0 and m_1 are constants

W_t is a unit-cost inflation factor for holding inventories.

Combining equations 7.7 and 7.9 gives

$$S_t^* = -\frac{m_0}{m_1} + \frac{PX_t}{m_1 W_t} + \frac{f(P_{t+1}/1+r_{t,t+1})}{m_1 W_t} + \left[\frac{W_{t+1}}{W_t(1+r_{t,t+1})}\right]$$

$$\times \left[\left(\sum_{i=1}^{4} b_{i+1} SQ_{i+1}\right)\right] - \frac{(\Sigma b_i SQ_i)}{m_1} + k_2 C_{t+1} \tag{7.10}$$

The optimal stock is thus a function of the expected cost reduction from holding inventories (including expected price differences and seasonal handling differences), the future price level (representing uncertainty) relative to an inventory cost factor, and next period's consumption.

Some generalization of equation 7.10 can be permitted by allowing for some error in attaining the optimal stock. Thus, deliveries at time t are

$$B_t = d \, (S_t^* - S_{t-1}) + C_t + E_t \tag{7.11}$$

where B_t is deliveries of coal at t

     d is between 0 and 1 and is a constant proportion of adjustment from the stock at the beginning of the period, S_{t-1} to the optimal stock this period, S_t

     E_t is a random element, independently distributed with an expected value of 0.

Using the fact that $B_t + S_{t-1} - C_t = S_t$, and combining equations 7.10 and 7.11 gives equation 7.12 for each state's stock of coal held by electric utilities for the data points where the constraint is not binding.

$$S_t = a_0 + a_1 PXW_t + a_2 PDW_t + a_3 WR_t + a_4 WR12_t + a_5 WR23_t$$

$$+ a_6 WR41_t + a_7 C_{t+1} + a_8 S_{t-1} + E_t \tag{7.12}$$

where $PXW_t = PX_t / W_t$
$PDW_t = P_{t+1} / W_t (1 + r_{t, t+1})$
$WR_t = W_{t+1} / W_t (1 + r_{t, t+1})$
$WR12_t = SQ1 \times WR_t - SQ2$
$WR23_t = SQ2 \times WR_t - SQ3$
$WR41 = SQ4 \times WR_t - SQ1$
$a = -(db_4 + m_0) / m_1 < 0$
$a_1 = d / m_1 > 0$
$a_2 = df / m_1 > 0$
$a_3 = db_4 / m_1 > 0$
$a_4 = d(b_2 - b_4) / m_1$
$a_5 = d(b_3 - b_4) / m_1$
$a_6 = d(b_1 - b_4) / m_1$
$a_7 = dk_2 > 0$
$a_8 = 1 - d < 1$

There are nine parameters in equation 7.12 and nine structural parameters in the model. Given the assumed restrictions on the structural parameters, then of the parameters in equation 7.12, a_0 should be negative; a_1, a_2, a_3, and a_7 should be positive; a_8 should be between 0 and 1; and a_4, a_5, and a_6 can be either positive or negative.

For the data points when the minimal stock constraint is binding, the stock is given by equation 7.13.

$$S_t = k_1 C_{t+1} + E'_t \tag{7.13}$$

where E'_t is random with expected value of zero and finite variance.

PRAGMATIC ALTERNATIVES AND THE DATA

There are many practical alterations necessary for the actual estimation for each state equation. The exogenous variables in equation 7.12 are PX_t, expected price change; W_t, unit cost escalation factor; the appropriate one-period interest rate; expected future consumption; and last period's stocks. Last period's stock is known and future consumption will be taken as exogenous to this model.

There are many alternative proxies for the expected future price, P_{t+1}. Assuming utilities know the values of Y_{t+1}, in equation 7.2, then the appropriate values for P_t over the period of estimation would be the fitted values from an estimated equation 7.2, where P_t is the price of coal to utilities in a state. Furthermore, as clearly pointed out by Gordon,[5] the price paid by a utility will depend upon whether the coal is from captive mines, bought on contract, or on-the-spot market; transportation costs; chemical content (water, ash, sulfur, and so on); and several other minor factors. Since virtually all coal contracts have escalation clauses and many are based upon national indexes and since relatively very little steam electric coal is captive,[6] first the actual values of the Wholesale Price Index for bituminous coal will be used. Since the regional price of coal is endogenous to the total supply–demand model, using actual values may appear to cause a simultaneous equation bias in estimating equation 7.12. However, practical experience teaches that this bias has little effect on the estimated parameters; the appropriate price variable is a regional price that would require modeling the amount under contract and the amount purchased on the spot market, and only when other aspects of the total supply–demand model are formalized could the equations for deliveries be reestimated fairly easily by using a better estimation technique such as two-stage least squares.

The second pragmatic alternative is to assume that virtually all electrical coal is purchased under contract in a particular state so that the expected price change, PX_t, is zero in equation 7.12. In this case, utilities would equate the marginal inventory storage cost with the discounted difference in seasonal handling costs. Since there are no data on either of these costs, they can be estimated only relatively. Thus, in this case, the structural parameter m_0 can be set equal to zero.

Whether the Wholesale Price Index of coal is used for PX_t or coal is purchased under contract and PX_t is not included in the equation, periods of strikes present problems. Around the periods of major coal strikes in 1968:4, 1971:4, and 1974:4, actual changes in the Wholesale Price Index for coal or the assumption that PX_t is zero would not reflect the expected costs of obtaining coal during and around the periods of the strikes. Thus, dummy variables will have to be added to equation 7.12 to reflect these deviations.

The appropriate variable for W_t in equation 7.12 is the unit-cost escalation factor corresponding to unit-cost increases for delivery, handling, and storing coal by electrical utilities. Here, again, deference to pragmatism and forecasting problems is important. Determining these actual costs would be a major research effort in itself. Then, a model would have to be developed to forecast these changes. An alternative would be to use unit labor costs for the entire economy or for all manufacturing as these variables are typically forecasted reasonably well by the large-scale macro-econometric models. At the aggregate level, however, these data are heavily affected by productivity changes over the business cycle and almost certainly do not relate to changes in unit costs for particular state utilities' handling of coal. A better method with regard to estimation would be to assume that unit costs are constant: that changes in factor costs have been just offset by changes in factor productivity. Thus, W_t can be set equal to 1 in equation 7.12.

For the interest-rate variable in the model, the prime rate should be an adequate proxy.

The dependent variable, S_t, is the quarterly average end-of-the-month stocks, in tons, held by electric utilities; and consumption of coal by electric utilities, C_t, is the quarterly consumption, both as reported on Form 4 filed with the Federal Power Commission. Data were collected from 1967 through the third quarter of 1975. Given one lagged variable and one led variable, the period of estimation is 1967:2 through 1975:2, or 33 observations.

A comparison of average quarterly deliveries with average stocks, as shown in Table 7.1, indicates that over the period 1967:2 to 1975:2, utilities generally held less than a one-quarter supply of coal. The preponderance of average stocks, especially for the states with electric utilities that use large amounts of coal, are between 73 and 90 days.

Incorporating the alterations discussed above gives the following equations:
for points where the constraint is binding,

$$S_t = k_1 C_{t+1} + E_t'; \qquad\qquad (7.13)$$

and for points where the constraint is not binding, either
(1) the wholesale price index is significant;

$$S_t = a_0 + a_1 PX_t + a_2 PCDR_t + a_3 D_t + a_4 D23_t + a_5 D41_t$$

$$+ a_6 D12_t + a_7 C_{t+1} + a_8 S_{t-1} + a_9 STK_t + E_t \qquad (7.14)$$

TABLE 7.1

Average Quarterly Supply of Coal Held by Electric Utilities
by State, 1967:2 to 1975:2

State or Region	Code	
Alabama	AL	.97
Colorado	CO	1.21
Delaware	DE	.69
Florida	FL	.59
Georgia	GA	.92
Illinois	IL	.84
Indiana	IN	.89
Iowa	IA	1.81
Kansas	KS	2.83
Kentucky	KY	.83
Michigan	MI	.99
Nebraska	NE	2.03
New Jersey	NJ	1.19
New York	NY	.79
Ohio	OH	.86
Pennsylvania	PA	.97
Tennessee	TN	.97
Virginia	VA	.85
West Virginia	WV	.97
Wisconsin	WI	1.22
New England	N	1.34
District of Columbia–Maryland	DM	.78
North Dakota–South Dakota–Minnesota–Montana	1	1.04
California–Nevada	NV	.46
New Mexico–Arizona	3	.48
Wyoming–Utah	4	.53
Arkansas–Mississippi–Missouri	5	.77
North Carolina–South Carolina	6	.82

Source: Compiled by the author.

where $PX_t = P_{t+1}/(1+r_{t,t+1}) - P_t$
       $PCDR_t = P_{t+1}/(1+r_{t,t+1})$
       $D_t = 1/1+r_{t,t+1}$
       $D23_t = SQ2 \times D_t - SQ3$
       $D41_t = SQ4 \times D_t \, SQ1$
       $D12_t = SQ1 \times D_t - SQ2$
       STK_t = dummy strike variables
       P_t = WPI for bituminous coal and lignite
       $r_{t,t+1}$ = Prime interest rate/400
       $a_0 - a_8$ are the same as for equation 7.12.

     (2) all coal purchased on long-term contract, therefore
        $PX_t = 0$, and
$$S_t = a_1 DMIN1_t + a_2 D23 + a_3 D41 + a_4 D12 + a_5 S_{t-1} \qquad (7.15)$$
$$+ a_6 C_{t+1} + a_7 STK_t + E_t$$

where $DMIN1 = 1/(1+r_{t,t+1}) - 1$

     D23, D41, D12, and STK_t are the same as in equation 7.14
     $a_1 = db_4/m_1 > 0$
     $a_2 = d(b_3 - b_4)/m_1$
     $a_3 = d(b_1 - b_4)/m_1$
     $a_4 = d(b_2 - b_4)/m_1$
     $a_5 = 1-d > 0$
     $a_6 = k_2 d > 0$.

There are two special cases that may occur: the rate of adjustment is one period and, thus, $d = 1$ and the coefficient for S_{t-1} is 0; there is change in capacity effect on marginal storage costs and thus the coefficient for C_{t+1} is 0.

ESTIMATING PROCEDURE

The final problem is the econometric estimation procedure appropriate for the switching regression model. Formally, maximum likelihood techniques can be employed to produce efficient and unbiased estimates as shown in Maddala and Nelson.[7] Such an approach has several problems: these iterative techniques are quite expensive; adding the strike dummy variables, which is mostly an art rather than a science, would be extremely difficult and multiply the time and cost of this effort enormously; there are probably not enough data points to apply maximum likelihood; and the treatment of autocorrelation in residuals is an insurmountable problem with these methods. Consequently, as a first step, either equations 7.14 or 7.15 will be estimated over the whole estimation period-- that is, the constraint will be assumed to be nonbinding; or equation

7.13 will be estimated over the entire period--that is, the constraint will be assumed to be always binding. In both cases, ordinary least squares (OLS) will be used. Autocorrelation of errors is a severe problem for models with lagged variables as it renders the OLS estimator both biased and inconsistent. Furthermore, the Durbin-Watson statistic is inappropriate for equations with lagged dependent variables. Durbin has suggested an alternative test to be used. [8] If there is evidence of serial correlation of errors then the equations will be rerun correcting for this.

EMPIRICAL RESULTS OF ORDINARY LEAST SQUARES

Equations 7.14 and 7.15 were run for the 28 states or groups of states. These results were satisfactory in terms of the signs of the coefficients and the standard error of the equation for all states except Florida and Nebraska. For those two states, the naive model, equation 7.16, was a better fit for the data.

$$S_t = a_0 + a_1 S_{t-1} + a_2 C_{t+1} + a_3 SQ1 + a_4 SQ2 + a_5 SQ3 \qquad (7.16)$$

$$+ a_6 Strike + E_t$$

where S_t is the stock of coal
C_t is the consumption of coal
SQ1, SQ2, and SQ3 are seasonal dummy variables
Strike is a strike dummy variable.

In no case was equation 7.13 superior. These results are summarized in Table 7.2. Equation 7.14, which contains the change in the WPI for coal, PX_t, was the best equation for 17 states or groups and equation 7.15 for the remaining 9 states or groups.

In the equations of Table 7.2 the absolute standard error ranges from a high of just over 500,000 tons per quarter for Ohio, 1.8 percent of quarterly deliveries, to 31,000 tons, 3.05 percent of Delaware's quarterly deliveries of coal to electric utilities.

All coefficients either had the correct sign or the equation was rejected. As might be expected, not all the seasonal difference in handling and unloading costs--variables D12, D23, and D41--were significantly different from zero. Generally, all other variables were significantly different from zero. (Details for each equation are available on request from the author.)

In all cases where equation 7.14 was the best equation, except one, the sign of the coefficient for PCDR was positive, indicating risk aversion that increases as the price of coal rises. Interestingly,

TABLE 7.2

Summary of Estimated Equations for Stocks Held by State Electric Utilities, 1967:2 to 1975:2

State or Region	Best Equation	R^2	h^a	Absolute Standard Error (1,000 tons)
Alabama	15	.9292	4.20b	343.4
Colorado	14	.9850	1.36	61.6
Delaware	14	.8548	-.33	31.1
Florida	16	.9008	--	85.0
Georgia	15	.9422	1.63	250.4
Illinois	15	.8175	.38	494.9
Indiana	14	.8743	.61	321.4
Iowa	15	.9519	2.48b	137.4
Kansas	14	.9789	.51	68.0
Kentucky	15	.9559	.61	368.8
Michigan	14	.9581	.13	232.6
Nebraska	16	.9241	3.73b	55.8
New Jersey	14	.6649	8.28b	97.0
New York	14	.9228	.02	160.6
Ohio	14	.9296	-.69	512.6
Pennsylvania	14	.9405	.09	469.5
Tennessee	15	.9546	2.68b	377.5
Virginia	14	.8523	1.19	94.3
West Virginia	14	.9684	.54	309.6
Wisconsin	15	.8767	1.46	279.1
New England	14	.9793	2.01b	116.9
Maryland-District of Columbia	14	.7981	-1.13	109.8
North Dakota- South Dakota- Minnesota- Montana	15	.9077	.02	246.1
Nevada	14	.9678	2.93b	34.9
New Mexico-Arizona	14	.9835	-.87	53.5
Wyoming-Utah	14	.9824	.64	64.8
Arkansas- Mississippi- Missouri	14	.9654	-2.23b	193.9
North Carolina- South Carolina	15	.8152	3.33b	437.9

^{a}h is the Durbin statistic for testing for autocorrelation when there are lagged dependent variables.

^{b}Indicates the hypothesis of zero autocorrelation would be rejected at the 5 percent level.

Source: Calculated by the author.

for Nevada the sign of the coefficient for PCDR was negative, indicating a preference for risk, or willingness to gamble, that increases as the price of coal increases.

The fourth column of Table 7.2 contains the Durbin h statistic, a test for autocorrelation when there are lagged dependent variables. This statistic has a standard normal distribution. Thus, one would reject the hypothesis of zero autocorrelation at the 5 percent level if h were greater than 1.65. Nine states or groups show evidence of autocorrelation. There are various methods to correct for this. One of the more sophisticated techniques has been suggested by Wallis.[9] Wallis suggests a generalized least-squares approach. However, for this particular problem this technique is too expensive and time consuming.

Instead, the degree of autocorrelation was approximated by calculating r for each equation as shown in equation 7.17.

$$r = 1 - .5D\text{-}W + k/n$$

where D-W is the Durbin-Watson statistic from the equations
　　　　summarized in Table 7.2
　　k is the number of parameters in the equations
　　n is equal to 32.
Given r, each equation was reestimated in the form given in equation 7.18.

$$(S_t - rS_{t-1}) = a_0 + a_1 (S_{t-1} - rS_{t-2}) + a_2 (X_t - rX_{t-1})$$

$$+ E_t \tag{7.18}$$

where S_t is the dependent variable, stocks
　　　X_t is the vector of independent variables in the equations.

Table 7.3 indicates the effect of the equations with a correction for autocorrelation. As expected, the R^2 is lower for each equation, since the dependent variable is $S_t - rS_{t-1}$. However, the absolute standard error of the regression was reduced by 25 to 3 percent: for Alabama, from 343,400 tons to 257,700 tons; and for New Jersey, from 97,000 tons to 93,700 tons.

For the Iowa equation, the sign on the variable DMIN1 became negative (although insignificant), which is inconsistent with the theory developed earlier in the section entitled "Theoretical Framework." Therefore, the naive model was run for Iowa and indicated that autocorrelation was present. With autocorrelation correction, the naive model does as well for Iowa as equation 7.15 (see Table 7.3).

TABLE 7.3

Comparison of Best Uncorrected Equation with
Equation Correct for Autocorrelation

State or Region	Old Equation		r^a	New Equation	
	R^2	Absolute Standard Error (1,000 tons)		R^2	Absolute Standard Error (1,000 tons)
Alabama	.9292	343.4	.92	.8765	257.7
Iowa[b]	.9519	137.4	.55	.9290	125.5
Iowa-naive	--	--	.55	.9282	126.2
Nebraska	.9241	55.8	.78	.9301	46.1
New Jersey	.6649	97.0	.69	.5252	93.7
Tennessee	.9546	377.5	.60	.9008	319.6
New England	.9793	116.9	.58	.8972	115.4
Nevada	.9678	34.9	.72	.9150	30.2
Arkansas-Mississippi-Missouri	.9654	193.9	-.62	.9890	171.5
North Carolina-South Carolina	.8152	437.9	.75	.6177	378.0

[a]Correction for autocorrelation as defined in the text.
[b]Variables became insignificant.
Source: Compiled by the author.

Of greater significance is the effect on the estimated coefficients for lagged stock and led consumption. The presence of positive autocorrelation in an uncorrected equation will bias the coefficient upward on the lagged dependent variable. Table 7.4 shows the
effect of autocorrelation correction. The coefficient for lagged
stock is lowered by as much as .2, from .434 to .226, for the states
that indicated positive autocorrelation. Table 7.4 also shows a significant change in the coefficients for led consumption. This is particularly important since in these models consumption is exogenous
for forecasting while lagged stock is endogenous after one quarter
into the forecast period.

TABLE 7.4

Change in Coefficients with Autocorrelation Correction

State or Region	S_{t-1}	C_{t+1}
Alabama		
Uncorrected	.908	.275
Corrected	.866	.286
Difference	-.042	+.011
Iowa		
Uncorrected	.961	.131
Corrected	.785	.388
Difference	-.176	+.257
Nebraska		
Uncorrected	.713	.359
Corrected	.552	.380
Difference	-.161	+.121
New Jersey		
Uncorrected	.434	.166
Corrected	.226	.253
Difference	-.208	+.087
Tennessee		
Uncorrected	.852	.469
Corrected	.698	.595
Difference	-.154	+.126
New England		
Uncorrected	.599	.647
Corrected	.589	.589
Difference	-.010	.058
Nevada		
Uncorrected	.286	.074
Corrected	.171	.105
Difference	-.115	+.031
Arkansas-Mississippi- Missouri		
Uncorrected	.603	.167
Corrected	.702	.060
Difference	+.099	-.107
North Carolina- South Carolina		
Uncorrected	.802	.293
Corrected	.697	.334
Difference	-.105	+.041

Source: Compiled by the author.

SUMMARY AND CONCLUSIONS

In this chapter a theoretical model of cost minimization under uncertainty for electric utilities holding stocks of coal was developed. It was assumed that utilities face a constraint of a minimal amount of coal they must hold. This theoretical model results in a "switching regression" type model since data points may lie on the marginal cost curve or the constraint curve. For this type of model, maximum likelihood techniques are appropriate. However, because of cost considerations and the practical problem of "fitting" data around strike periods, this technique was rejected. Several other practical assumptions were required to make the theoretical model operational. The most important of these were the appropriateness of national price indexes for the cost of coal to utilities and the changes in unit costs.

The model was estimated regionally for 28 states or groups of states. The results of the estimation procedure were relatively good. The theoretical model was acceptable for all states and groups but two, where a naive model performed as well or better. The standard errors of the estimating equations as a percentage of the mean ranged from 1.8 to 3.05 percent. Nine equations indicated autocorrelation problems as measured by the Durbin h statistic. The correction for this improved the accuracy for these equations. However, the Iowa equation when corrected for autocorrelation had an improper sign and the naive model was substituted.

While a relatively good set of equations has been developed here for forecasting deliveries of coal to electric utilities given consumption of coal, there are a number of limitations and improvements that could be made with more time and monies invested. In particular, regional prices (costs) should be used, contract purchases of coal versus spot purchases should be modeled, and the effects of strikes should be modeled. Each of these is important but it is also complex and expensive. For a short-run econometric model, the net benefits of this detail are problematical. For a longer-term model, a more structured approach to both the supply and demand for coal would be necessary.

NOTES

1. R. L. Gordon, "Optimization of Input Supply Patterns in the Case of Fuels for Electric Power Generation," Journal of Industrial Economics 23 (September 1974): 19-37.

2. H. Averch and L. Johnson, "Behavior of the Regulated Firm," American Economic Review 52 (December 1962): 1052-69.

3. R. A. Meyer, "Capital Structure and the Behavior of the Regulated Firm under Uncertainty," Southern Economic Journal 42 (April 1976): 600–09.

4. Y. Peles and J. Stein, "The Effect of Rate of Return Regulation is Highly Sensitive to the Nature of Uncertainty," American Economic Review 66 (June 1976): 278–89.

5. Gordon, op. cit.

6. Ibid.

7. G. S. Maddala and F. D. Nelson, "Switching Regression Models with Endogenous and Exogenous Switching," American Statistical Association Proceedings, December 1975.

8. J. Durbin, "Testing for Serial Correlation in Least-Squares Regression When Some of the Regressors are Lagged Dependent Variables," Econometrica 38 (1970): 410–21.

9. K. F. Wallis, "Lagged Dependent Variables and Serially Correlated Errors: A Reappraisal of Three-Pass Least Squares," Review of Economics and Statistics, 1967, pp. 555–67.

8

OMITTED CROSS-SECTIONAL
EFFECTS IN MEASUREMENT OF
ECONOMIES OF SCALE IN
ELECTRICITY GENERATION
Gurmukh S. Gill

The area of generation costs is perhaps the most extensively studied part of cost functions in electricity supply econometrics. (See Galatin for a survey.[1] Subsequent to this survey there have been a number of studies done at Berkeley under the supervision of D. McFadden.) Though this literature is very extensive, the estimates of the parameters are often obtained from cross-sectional data and the nature of the biases produced by unobservable and omitted cross-sectional effects is not known. (See Friedman[2] for a strong critique of measurement of economies of scale from cross-section data.) The purpose of this chapter is to throw some light on this issue.

There are, broadly speaking, two kinds of studies that have been done until now. One is the set of studies that relate costs (fuel, labor, capital, production expenses, total costs, and so on) to output, capacity (or load factor), and other factors like vintage dummies. These are the studies by Nordin, Lomax, Johnston, Komiya, Barzel, Galatin and Ling (see Galatin for a survey). The other is the set of

---

Research sponsored by the National Science Foundation RANN Program and the U.S. Energy Research and Development Administration under Union Carbide Corporation's contract with the U.S. Energy Research and Development Administration, Oak Ridge National Laboratory, Oak Ridge, Tennessee.

Programming assistance provided by S. M. Cohn is gratefully acknowledged. Assistance provided by Mary Ann Griffin and Michael Zimmer in collecting data is appreciated. I would also like to thank G. S. Maddala for suggesting the topic and for many helpful comments.

studies that follow Nerlove's[3] lead and, using the duality theory, derive a cost function where total costs are a function of output and input prices. Though the latter approach is theoretically more appealing (see, however, Galatin for a critique), as Nerlove pointed out, the measurement of the capital component of costs and of capital "price" poses the greatest difficulties. Hence we will be estimating input demand functions as was done by Barzel and Galatin. Our purpose is to illustrate the nature of biases that arise from omitted cross-sectional effects and the same type of analysis can be done for the type of cost function estimation done by Nerlove and a generalization of his model to the translog cost function. We will, in subsequent sections, discuss separately the equations for fuel input, labor input, production expenses, and capital input.

FUEL INPUT EQUATIONS

To abstract from problems arising from differences in fuel prices, we take physical measures of fuel input. The dependent variable is fuel input in Btu per unit of output--a measure often known as the heat rate. Since we wanted to investigate the most recent data, we estimated a cross-section equation for 1972 using plant data. The data are from the Federal Power Commission (FPC)[4] and cover 544 plants. Plants containing additions and deletions in that year have been omitted. Separate vintage dummies were defined for these years: pre-1953, 1954-56, 1957-59, 1960-62, 1963-65, 1966-68, 1969-71. Also, another dummy was defined for coal and noncoal plants. Define HR = heat rate, X = output, and C = capacity. The estimated equation (t-ratios in parentheses) was:

$$\text{Ln HR} - \text{Constant } -.159 \text{ Ln X} + .093 \text{ Ln C} + \text{Dummies}$$
$$(-14.3) \qquad (7.8)$$
$$R^2 = .6756 \qquad (8.1)$$

This equation shows substantial economies of scale in the fuel output. Since HR = fuel input/x, the elasticity of fuel input with respect to output is given by $1 - 0.159 = .0841$. The positive coefficient of Ln C in equation 8.1 can be explained as follows:

Define PF = plant factor. Then we can write the fuel input per unit of output as:*

---

*Throughout our analysis we did not use any input prices in the demand functions. Essentially, we are assuming a fixed coefficient production function as Komiya did.[5] If we allow for input

$$HR = AC^{\alpha} (PF)^{\beta}$$

We would expect $\alpha < 0$ and $\beta < 0$. Since PF is proportional to $\dfrac{X}{C}$ we have

$$HR = \text{Constant } C^{\alpha} \left(\dfrac{X}{C}\right)^{\beta}$$

$$= \text{Constant } C^{\alpha - \beta} X^{\beta} \qquad\qquad (8.2)$$

Comparing this with equation 1 we have

$$\hat{\alpha} - \hat{\beta} = .093 \text{ and } \hat{\beta} = -.159 \text{ or } \hat{\alpha} = -.066$$

Thus, both the coefficients in 8.1 have the expected signs. *

Though the vintage dummies and fuel dummies do take account of some important characteristics of the plants, there may be many other plant-specific factors that they do not capture. These include physical characteristics of the plant and managerial and operating ability. One rather drastic way of accounting for these factors is to estimate the equations in first differences. If we write the equation for heat rate as

$$H_{it} = A X_{it}^{\alpha} \ C_{it}^{\beta} \ S_i \gamma e \delta^{t} \qquad\qquad (8.3)$$

where S_t = the error term

$\quad H_{it}$ = the heat rate for plant i at time t

$\quad X_{it}$ = the output for plant i at time t

$\quad C_{it}$ = the capacity of plant i at time t

$\quad S_i$ = the composite measure of all factors specific to plant i

then, if we consider plants with no capacity changes, we have, taking first differences of the logs,

$$\Delta \text{Log } H_{it} = \text{Constant} + \alpha \Delta \text{ Log } X_{it}$$

We estimated this equation on the basis of data for 510 plants for the years 1971 and 1972. These plants had no capacity changes during these years. The estimated equation was:

---

substitution, we have to bring in the prices of fuel input as well as those of labor and capital. Here our purpose is to illustrate the point about neglected cross-sectional effects.
    *The standard error of $\hat{\alpha}$ was 0.004.

$$\Delta \text{Log } H = .0018 - .0067 \ \Delta \text{Log } X \qquad R^2 = .1758 \qquad (8.4)$$
$$(1.2) \qquad (-10.4)$$

Comparing the results of equation 8.4 with those in 8.1 we note that the elasticity of fuel input with respect to output has increased from around 0.84 to around 0.933. The positive intercept term in 8.4 indicates that there has been an overall deterioration in heat rates (possibly due to environmental controls or to more generation at off-design conditions).

An alternative approach to account for these plant-specific characteristics is to estimate equation 8.3 from pooled cross-section time-series data. However, there are problems if we have some capacity changes in between because the reported output is for different levels of capacity in that year. Hence, we chose 134 plants which did not have any capacity changes during the 1968-72 period. The total number of plants that had no capacity changes during this period is higher than this but we omitted some plants which are very old and some which are very small (the list of plants included is available on request). We estimated the equations using six vintage dummies and a fuel-code dummy, which was defined as 1 for a coal plant, 0 otherwise. Vintages were 1966-67, 1964-65, 1962-63, 1960-61, 1958-59, and 1957 and before. The results for the individual years are presented in Table 8.1.

TABLE 8.1

Dependent Variable: Ln (Heat Rate)

Year	Ln (output)	Ln (capacity)	Ln (no. of units)	R^2
1968	−.089 (5.2)	.0182 (1.0)	.0683 (6.8)	.5931
1969	−.106 (5.6)	.0335 (1.7)	.0674 (6.1)	.5744
1970	−.085 (4.5)	.0112 (0.6)	.0700 (6.5)	.5370
1971	−.102 (5.0)	.0267 (1.2)	.0686 (6.0)	.5138
1972	−.084 (4.9)	.0098 (0.6)	.0712 (6.3)	.4825

Note: Vintage and fuel dummies not reported. Figures in parentheses are t-ratios.

Source: Compiled by the author.

These results indicate an elasticity of fuel input with respect to output of around 0.9. For the same data, regression in first differences of the form

$$\Delta \text{Ln HR} = \alpha + \beta \Delta \text{ Ln X} \qquad (8.5)$$

gave the following results:

Year	β	R^2
1968-69	-.0799 (6.9)	.2657
1969-70	-.0711 (3.9)	.1064
1970-71	-.0427 (2.9)	.0616
1971-72	-.0571 (5.5)	.1865

Also, the estimation from pooled cross-section and time-series data with cross-section and time dummies gave the following results:

$$\text{Ln HR} = 9.633 - 0.0522 \text{ Ln X} \qquad (8.6)$$
$$(-11.1)$$

which implies an elasticity of fuel input with respect to output of 0.95.

In conclusion, if we estimate cross-sectional equations using vintage dummies and fuel dummies, the elasticities of fuel input with respect to output are around 0.85 if we include all the plants, and around 0.90 if we exclude very old and very small plants. On the other hand, if we make allowance for all plant-specific effects either by estimating the equations from first-difference form or by estimating them from pooled cross-section and time-series data with plant dummies, this elasticity is around 0.95, thus reducing the magnitude of economies of scale.

PRODUCTION EXPENSES AND EMPLOYMENT

For the same set of 134 plants discussed in the previous section, we estimated equations for production expenses. The results are shown in Table 8.2.

The estimates from pooled-time series and cross-section data with plant and year dummies were:*

$$\text{Ln PE} = 5.002 - .4590 \text{ Ln X} \qquad (8.7)$$
$$(18.6) \quad (-13.6)$$

---

*Since the equations were in log form and time dummies were included, we did not have to deflate production expenses.

TABLE 8.2

Dependent Variable: Ln (Production Expense/Kwh)

Year	Ln (output)	Ln (capacity)	Ln (no. of units)	R^2
1968	-.2113 (2.2)	.1220 (1.1)	.051 (0.9)	.1707
1969	-.3253 (3.3)	.2074 (2.0)	.061 (1.0)	.2212
1970	-.3275 (2.6)	.2168 (1.7)	.041 (0.6)	.1791
1971	-.1902 (1.2)	.1104 (0.7)	.041 (0.5)	.0859
1972	-.3136 (2.4)	.2477 (1.9)	.016 (0.1)	.0970

Note: Vintage and fuel dummies not reported.
Source: Compiled by the author.

In the case of production expense the elasticity from the pooled equation is lower (about 1-0.459 or 0.54) than from the individual cross-sectional equations. To understand this we have to look at the employment equations.

The results of the employment equations for this set of plants are given in Table 8.3.

TABLE 8.3

Dependent Variable: Average Number of Employees

Year	Ln (output)	Ln (capacity)	Ln (no. of units)	R^2
1968	.4553 (2.8)	.1643 (2.0)	.3373 (4.2)	.6292
1969	.4184 (2.6)	.2121 (2.3)	.3153 (3.9)	.6143
1970	.3829 (2.0)	.2495 (2.3)	.3188 (3.8)	.6006
1971	.4190 (2.2)	.2263 (2.1)	.3487 (4.2)	.6213
1972	.3676 (2.0)	.2879 (2.9)	.2815 (3.3)	.6004

Note: Vintage and fuel dummies not reported.
Source: Compiled by the author.

The estimates from pooled cross-section time-series with plant and year dummies (not reported here) were:

$$\text{Ln } E = 3.902 + 0.1017 \text{ LN } X$$
$$(17.6) \quad (3.8) \tag{8.8}$$

What this result says is that given the plant capacity, changes in output require very little changes in employment. A 10 percent increase in output requires only a 1 percent increase in employment. The results of the previous section show that a 10 percent increase in output requires almost a 10 percent increase in fuel input. These figures together explain the result obtained earlier that the elasticity of production expense with respect to output is of the order of 0.54.

The equations for fuel input, labor input, and production expense we have estimated are perhaps very crude but they can be justified under a fixed production coefficient framework. However, they do give quite plausible estimates of the elasticities of fuel and labor inputs with respect to output holding capacity constant. The results also point out some drawbacks in making inferences about economies of scale from pure cross-section studies.

CAPITAL COSTS

One of the major problems with the estimation of cost functions with total costs as the dependent variables is the problem of how to treat capital costs. The cost data reported in the FPC reports are actual and historical costs. Over the years there is very little change in the reported costs of equipment throughout the life of any given plant. If a plant has different units added in different years, the historical and actual costs of the respective years of addition are just added up. Ling took the historical costs reported and, since these costs comprised units of various sizes and years of installation, he deflated them by a weighted cost index with respect to the year of installation of each unit.[6] He then took 12 percent of this figure as the capital cost. This procedure does not take account of depreciation of the plant over time.

Since the reported capital costs pose several problems, to get some insights into economies of scale, if any, in capital costs, we took the capital costs for each plant during the first year of its operation and related it to its capacity. Additions of units to existing plants were also considered. The equations estimated were:

$$\text{Ln (EQC)} = \alpha + \beta_1 \text{ Ln } C + \beta_2 \text{ Ln PSI} + \beta_3 D_1 + \beta_4 + D_2$$

$$+ \beta_5 D_3 \tag{8.9}$$

where   EQC = equipment cost in dollars
     C   = capacity
     PSI   = steam pressure
     D_1 = 1 if it is a coal plant
            = 0 otherwise
     D_2 = 1 if it is conventional
            = 0 otherwise (outdoor, semioutdoor)
     D_3 = 1 if plant is new
            = 0 if the units are added to an existing plant.

The same equation was also estimated with equipment cost per unit rather than total equipment cost as the dependent variable.

In all, there were 753 additions during the 1952-72 period that we considered. Additions for which capital cost data were not available or were found defective were omitted.

The data were grouped into two- or three-year periods and no deflators were used. The grouping was done merely to increase the number of observations in each group. There could be some bias arising from the fact that deflators were not used but it is not unreasonable to assume that equipment costs did not change appreciably within each time span (of two or three years).

Table 8.4 presents the results with Ln (equipment costs) as the dependent variable. N is the number of observations in the group. Table 8.5 presents the results with Ln (equipment cost per unit) as the dependent variable. One general conclusion that can be drawn from these results (particularly those in Table 8.5, which are the most relevant ones because the number of units is taken into account) is that there are economies of scale in capital costs and that these have not diminished in recent years (see the results for 1970-72). It is true that equipment costs have as a whole risen in recent years, but this is not the same thing as saying that economies of scale do not exist anymore. *

A pooled regression with separate time dummies for each year gave the following results (the equipment costs were not deflated because the dependent variable is in the log form and the time dummies will pick up the effects of the deflators):

The second equation (which again is the more relevant one because it takes the number of units into account) shows the extent of economies of scale in capital costs (the coefficient of Ln C is significantly less than one). The time dummies (1952-53 = 0) were almost all positive except for the year 1972. The time dummies pick

---

*One has to be careful not to confuse shifts in the cost function with movements along a cost function.

TABLE 8.4

Dependent Variable: Ln (Equipment Cost)

Year	Constant	Ln C	Ln PSI	D_1	D_2	D_3	R^2	n
1952–54	5.012 (5.2)	.965 (7.3)	−.008 (−.1)	−.024 (−.1)	−.387 (−2.4)	.546 (3.9)	.4386	118
1955–56	5.627 (3.5)	.720 (6.9)	.064 (.2)	−.139 (−1.4)	−.075 (−.8)	.287 (3.1)	.7436	74
1957–58	1.667 (.7)	.780 (4.3)	.536 (1.3)	−.500 (−3.0)	.277 (1.7)	.434 (2.7)	.5837	104
1959–60	8.718 (3.0)	1.095 (5.6)	−.596 (−1.2)	−.062 (−.4)	−.091 (−.6)	.412 (2.6)	.4541	101
1961–62	5.002 (5.0)	.869 (11.7)	.052 (.3)	−.159 (−2.2)	.140 (2.0)	.105 (1.3)	.8417	70
1963–64	3.900 (4.0)	.891 (11.7)	.165 (1.0)	−.220 (−2.8)	.024 (.3)	.261 (3.3)	.8915	62
1965–67	3.910 (1.2)	1.153 (4.6)	−.072 (−.1)	−.006 (−.1)	.011 (.1)	.263 (1.3)	.5328	71
1968–69	2.537 (.7)	1.561 (4.9)	−.202 (−.3)	−.358 (−1.4)	−.097 (−.4)	.690 (2.5)	.6537	68
1970–72	8.116 (3.5)	.908 (4.6)	−.359 (−.9)	−.372 (−2.5)	.041 (.3)	.2825 (1.6)	.5430	85

Note: t−statistics are in parentheses.
Source: Compiled by the author.

TABLE 8.5

Dependent Variable: Ln (Equipment Cost/Unit)

Year	Constant	Ln C	Ln PSI	D_1	D_2	D_3	R^2	n
1952–54	5.416	.776	.045	-.074	-.310	.477	.3309	118
	(5.6)	(6.4)	(.3)	(-.5)	(-2.0)	(3.3)		
1955–56	4.309	.595	.313	-.127	-.029	.229	.7503	74
	(3.1)	(7.2)	(1.4)	(-1.5)	(-.4)	(2.7)		
1957–58	1.822	.726	.546	-.512	.293	.400	.5315	104
	(.9)	(4.2)	(1.6)	(-3.0)	(1.8)	(2.5)		
1959–60	6.122	.819	-.077	-.070	-.068	.381	.3816	101
	(2.4)	(4.9)	(-.2)	(-.5)	(-.5)	(2.4)		
1961–62	5.235	.812	.053	-.131	.153	.091	.7582	70
	(5.9)	(9.8)	(.4)	(-1.8)	(2.2)	(1.1)		
1963–64	3.546	.754	.302	-.253	.036	.231	.8627	62
	(4.3)	(10.0)	(2.2)	(-3.4)	(.5)	(3.2)		
1965–67	2.130	.960	.294	-.005	.021	.272	.4840	71
	(.7)	(4.1)	(.6)	(-.1)	(.1)	(1.4)		
1968–69	-2.361	.993	.848	.327	-.110	.605	.6369	68
	(-.7)	(3.5)	(1.3)	(1.2)	(-.5)	(2.1)		
1970–72	6.746	.769	-.079	-.363	.013	.296	.5627	85
	(2.9)	(4.2)	(-.2)	(-2.4)	(.1)	(1.7)		

Note: t-statistics are in parentheses.
Source: Compiled by the author.

up the effects of the price deflator as well as the effects of quality changes in the equipment over time. Thus, though the price index has been rising over time, the quality improvement in equipment more than compensated for price changes before 1972 (as compared with the base period 1952-53). The positive coefficient

$$\text{Ln (EQC)} = 4.518 + .947 \text{ LnC} + .077 \text{ Ln PSI} - .139 \text{ D}_1$$
$$\quad\quad\quad (8.3)\quad\ (19.2)\quad\quad (.8)\quad\quad\quad (-2.5)$$

$$-.009 \text{ D}_2 + .396 \text{ D}_3 + \text{Time Dummies}$$
$$(-.2)\quad\quad (7.3)$$
$$R^2 = .639, \text{ d.f.} = 728$$

$$\text{Ln (EQC/unit)} = 4.052 + .821 \text{ Ln C} + .211 \text{ Ln PSI}$$
$$\quad\quad\quad\quad\ (7.8)\quad\ (17.5)\quad\quad (2.5)$$

$$-.156 \text{ D}_1 + .010 \text{ D}_2 + .379 \text{ D}_3 + \text{Time Dummies}$$
$$(-2.9)\quad\quad (.2)\quad\quad (7.0)$$
$$R^2 = .622, \text{ d.f.} = .728$$

for the dummy variable in 1972 indicates that by that year quality adjusted equipment costs were for the first time higher than in 1952-53. However, this conclusion has to be qualified to the extent that we had to omit many additions made in 1972 due to lack of adequate cost data. When more data become available it would be possible to reestimate this equation as well as a cross-sectional equation for 1972 separately.

CONCLUSIONS

This chapter presents some evidence on the issue of economies of scale in electricity generation on the basis of cost data for recent years. The study estimates elasticities of fuel input, labor input, and production expenses with respect to output. The separate estimation of input demand functions is justified if we assume a fixed-coefficients model as Komiya had done. The results indicate that there are almost no economies of scale in the use of fuel input and that there are substantial economies of scale in the use of labor input.

The study also analyzes data on equipment costs for additions of equipment made during the 1952-72 period. Here the results show that there are economies of scale in capital costs (the elasticity of equipment cost with respect to capacity being around 0.82) and that these economies have not diminished during recent years. Though equipment costs, as a whole, have risen markedly during recent years, this is to be interpreted as an upward shift in the cost function and not as diseconomies of scale which refer to movements along a cost function. The pooled regression model with time dummies that we estimated for equipment cost data indicates that it is only very recently that the increases in equipment costs have not been adequately compensated by improvements in its quality. It is customary to quote the Handy-Whitman index to argue that equipment costs in electricity generation have risen faster than the wholesale price index. Ohta, using data until 1965, computed the quality adjusted cost index for generation equipment and found that equipment costs have actually fallen relative to the wholesale price index.[7] Since the dummies in the pooled regression model that we estimated pick up changes both in prices and in quality of equipment, our results confirm the results obtained by Ohta and indicate that equipment costs adjusted for quality changes have not risen as shown by the Handy-Whitman index except during very recent years.

One other important conclusion that stems from the analysis is that in studying the problem of economies of scale, one should use pooled cross-section and time-series data so that some firm-specific or plant-specific factors are taken into account. Discussions of economies of scale have been until now mostly based on results obtained from cross-section studies.

NOTES

1. M. Galatin, Economies of Scale and Technological Change in Thermal Power Generation (Amsterdam: North Holland Publishing Co., 1968).

2. M. Friedman, Comment on a paper by Caleb Smith in Business Concentration and Price Policy (Princeton, N.J.: National Bureau of Economic Research, 1955), pp. 230-38.

3. M. Nerlove, "Returns to Scale in Electricity Supply," in Measurement in Economics, Studies in Mathematical Economics and Econometrics in Memory of Yehuda Grunfed (Stanford, Calif.: Stanford University Press, 1963).

4. Federal Power Commission, Steam-Electric Plant Construction Cost and Annual Production Expenses, various issues.

5. R. Komiya, "Technical Progress and the Production Function in the U.S. Steam Power Industry," Review of Economics and Statistics, May 1962, pp. 156-66.

6. S. Ling, Economies of Scale in the Steam-Electric Power Generating Industry (Amsterdam: North Holland Publishing Co., 1964).

7. M. Ohta, "Production Technologies of the U.S. Boiler and Turbo Generator Industries and Hedonic Price Indexes of Their Products: A Cost Function Approach," Journal of Political Economy, February 1975, pp. 1-27.

9

EMPIRICAL TESTS OF THE
AVERCH-JOHNSON HYPOTHESIS:
A CRITICAL APPRAISAL
Michael A. Zimmer

During recent years there have been many empirical studies
on the effectiveness of rate of return regulation in the electric utility industry. The purpose of this chapter is to examine critically
these empirical studies. The sections of the chapter will review
the well-known Averch-Johnson hypothesis, the work on empirical
tests of this hypothesis, and the measures of rental price of capital
used in these studies. Since the cost of capital plays a fundamental
role in the analysis of regulation, the rental price of capital is a
crucial variable in the analysis. It will be argued that the empirical
studies on regulation have neglected this issue and used a variety of
proxy measures. A fifth section discusses the empirical method-
ologies and econometric specification in these studies, while the
final section presents the conclusion.

THE AVERCH-JOHNSON HYPOTHESIS

The simple model of a profit-maximizing firm subject to rate
of return regulation was first analyzed by Averch and Johnson (1962).
The most significant conclusion of the Averch-Johnson analysis is
that the effectively regulated firm maximizes profits by choosing a
capital-labor ratio which exceeds the ratio that would be chosen in

---

This chapter is based on my doctoral dissertation submitted
to the University of Tennessee. I would like to thank Professors
Sidney Carroll, Errol Glustoff, Harry Johnson, Feng-Yao Lee,
G. S. Maddala, John Moore, and Keith Phillips for helpful comments
at several stages.

the absence of regulation at that level of output. A brief examination of the model illustrates the distorted choice of inputs. Let

Q $= \Phi(K, L) =$ the firm's (well-behaved) production function
R(Q) $=$ the firm's total revenue function
K $=$ the amount of capital input
L $=$ $=$ the amount of labor input
P_K $=$ the implicit rental price per unit of capital
P_L $=$ the unit price of labor
s $=$ the allowed rate of return (assumed to exceed the cost
         of capital).

The firm seeks to maximize profits

$$R(Q) - P_L L - P_K K$$

subject to the rate of return and production constraints,

$$R(Q) - P_L L \leqq sK$$

$$Q \leqq \Phi(K, L)$$

The Lagrangean expression is given by

$$Z = R(Q) - P_L L - P_K K - \lambda \ R(Q) - P_L L - sK$$
$$- \Theta\{Q - \Phi(K, L)\} \tag{9.1}$$

Differentiation of equation 9.1 with respect to the choice variables Q, K, and L yields the necessary conditions for profit maxi-
mization:

$$R'(1-\lambda) - \Theta \leqq 0 \tag{9.2}$$
$$- P_K + \lambda s + \Theta \Phi_K \leqq 0 \tag{9.3}$$
$$- P_L(1-\lambda) + \Theta \Phi_L \leqq 0 \tag{9.4}$$
$$\Theta \geqq 0, \ \lambda \geqq 0, \ Q \geqq 0, \ K \geqq 0, \ L \geqq 0$$
$$\lambda R(Q) - P_L L - sK \ = 0$$
$$\Theta Q - \Phi(K, L) \ \ = 0$$

where subscripts on the symbol Φ denote partial derivatives of the
production function and R' denotes the derivative of the revenue
function with respect to Q.

If we assume that the problem has a solution at a positive level of output, then equations 9.2-9.4 are satisfied as equalities. Substituting for Θ in 9.3 and 9.4 yields

$$\Phi K / \Phi L = P'_K / P_L$$

where $P'_K = (P_K - \lambda s) / (1 - \lambda)$.

Thus the ratio of the marginal products is equal to the ratio of input prices (that is, the choice of inputs is efficient) only if $\lambda = 0$ (that is, only if the regulatory constraint is not binding). If $\lambda \neq 0$, then the choice of inputs is inefficient; it can be shown that the capital-labor ratio chosen in this case exceeds that which maximizes profit in the absence of regulation.[1]

This overcapitalization, often referred to as the Averch-Johnson thesis, results from an effective subsidy to capital in the form of a positive difference between the allowed rate of return and the market cost of capital. Since regulation is in terms of the rate of return on the firm's stock of productive capital, the firm will maximize its profits by using a larger capital-labor ratio than the unregulated firm.

EMPIRICAL TESTS OF THE AVERCH-JOHNSON HYPOTHESIS

Despite the potential importance of the Averch-Johnson thesis for energy policy, it is only within the past two years that empirical studies have appeared. The first to appear were by Courville (1974) and Spann (1974). These were followed by Petersen (1975), Cowing (1975), and, most recently, Hayashi and Trapani (1976) and Boyes (1976).

Courville, recognizing that one implication of the Averch-Johnson model is that the ratio of the marginal products of capital and a noncapital input is less than the ratio of their respective prices, attempts to estimate the marginal rate of technical substitution between capital and fuel for purposes of comparison with the price ratio.

The specification chosen for estimation is a modified Cobb-Douglas production function

$$\ln Q = \ln A + \alpha_K \ln K + \alpha_F \ln F + \alpha_L \ln L + \alpha_U U + \alpha_C F + \epsilon$$

where Q is output; K, L, and F are capital, labor, and fuel inputs, respectively; U is a measure of capacity utilization (the ratio of output to capacity); C is capacity; ϵ is a random disturbance term.

In the context of this production function, the ratio of the marginal products of capital and fuel can be written as

$$\alpha_K F / \alpha_F K$$

and the test for overcapitalization may be carried out by determining the sign of the expression

$$\alpha_K F / \alpha_F K - P_K / P_F$$

A negative value is taken as evidence supporting overcapitalization. Courville conducts the test by specifying the null hypothesis

$$\alpha_K F / K - \alpha_F P_K / P_F = 0 \tag{9.5}$$

and the alternate hypothesis

$$\alpha_K F / K - \alpha_F P_P / P_F < 0 \tag{9.6}$$

His data consist of annual observations on 110 new steam–electric generating plants for the periods 1948–50, 1951–55, 1956–59, and 1960–66. Each observation is taken from the first full year of plant operation. Estimating by single–equation least squares, Courville rejects the null hypothesis (equation 9.5) in favor of the alternative hypothesis (equation 9.6) for 105 of the 110 observations in the sample. He concludes that the evidence confirms the existence of overcapitalization.

The Spann study is an attempt at direct estimation of λ, the Lagrange multiplier associated with the regulatory constraint in the Averch–Johnson model. A nonzero value of λ implies that the regulatory constraint is binding, that is, that overcapitalization is present. Using a three–input transcendental logarithmic production function and restrictions implied by the first–order conditions of the Averch–Johnson model, Spann derives revenue share equations for the capital and fuel inputs:

$$S_K = b_1 + b_2 \ln K + b_3 \ln F + b_4 \ln L + \lambda Z \tag{9.7}$$

$$S_F = b_5 + b_6 \ln K + b_7 \ln F + b_8 \ln L \tag{9.8}$$

where, in addition to previously defined symbols, F denotes fuel; S_K and S_F represent the respective ratios of capital and fuel expenditures to total revenue R, and $Z = sK/R$, where s is the allowed rate of return.

Recognizing that equations 9.7 and 9.8 imply the interequation restriction

$$(1-\lambda)\ b_6 = b_3$$

Spann uses a nonlinear search procedure to estimate equations 9.7 and 9.8 and the coefficient λ. The system is estimated under the alternative restrictions

$(1-\lambda)\ b_6 = b_3$ and $b_6 = b_3$, which imply $\lambda \neq 0$ and $\lambda = 0$ respectively.

If it is determined that $\lambda \neq 0$, then overcapitalization may be inferred. Using plant-level data for the period 1959-63 and firm-level data for 1963, Spann is able to reject the null hypothesis $\lambda = 0$ at the .01 significance level; he concludes that regulation is effective.

Petersen bases his study on a cost minimization model with output assumed to be exogenous. Using a transcendental logarithmic cost function, he derives a cost share equation of the capital input,

$$P_K K/C = a_0 + a_1 \ln Q + a_2 (\ln Q)^2 + a_3 \ln P_K + a_c \ln P_F$$

$$+ a_5 \ln P_L + a_6 \ln(s - P_K) \qquad\qquad (9.9)$$

where all symbols are as defined before and C represents total production cost.

From the cost function Petersen derives two testable implications of the Averch-Johnson thesis, namely, that the derivatives of both total cost and the capital-cost share equation with respect to the allowed rate of return, s, are negative. Using ordinary least squares and estimating the cost function and equation 9.9 separately, he finds that these derived implications are confirmed by the statistical results. The sample consists of 56 steam generating plants which had experienced capacity increases of 50 percent or more during the period 1960-65. Observations used in estimation are taken from 1966, 1967, and 1968. The sample includes information on those states with and without regulation on a statewide basis, and on the method of rate base valuation (that is, "fair value" versus "original cost") in each state. Dummy variables are accordingly included in the estimating equations, and it is found that in each case the "state" variable is significant while the "valuation" variable is not significant. Petersen concludes that rate of return regulation is effective and that changes in the allowed rate of return significantly affect the degree of cost inefficiency attendant to the regulatory constraint.

Cowing analyzes regulatory effectiveness through the use of a system of equations comprising a generalized quadratic specification of the regulated profit function and the derived demand equations which are obtained by the use of Hotelling's Lemma for profit functions:[2]

$$\pi = a + b_0 P_K + b_1 P_F + b_2 P_L + b_3 s + (1/2) b_4 P_F{}^2$$

$$+ (1/2) b_5 P_L{}^2 + (1/2) b_6 P_K{}^2 + (1/2) b_7 s^2 + b_8 (P_F P_L)$$

$$+ b_9 (P_F P_K) + b_{10} (P_F s) + b_{11} (P_K P_L) \quad b_{12} (P_L s)$$

$$+ b_{13} (P_K s)$$

$$\partial \pi / \partial P_F = F^* = b_1 + b_4 P_F + b_8 P_L + b_9 P_K + b_{10} s$$

$$\partial \pi / \partial P_L = L^* = b_2 + b_5 P_L + b_8 P_F + b_{11} P_L + b_{12} s$$

$$\partial \pi / \partial P_K = K^* = b_0 + b_6 P_K + b_9 P_F + b_{11} P_L + b_{13} s$$

$$\partial \pi / \partial s \quad = b_3 + b_7 s + b_{10} P_F + b_{12} P_L + b_{13} P_K \qquad (9.10)$$

where all symbols are as defined before and the starred notation represents profit maximizing amounts of the three inputs.

Using a revision of Hotelling's Lemma to account for the presence of the regulatory constraint, Cowing derives a nonlinear system of equations equivalent to equation 9.10; the test for general regulatory effectiveness is conducted by estimating first the nonlinear system under the restriction

$$b_3 = b_7 = b_{10} = b_{12} = b_{13} = 0$$

and then with no restrictions imposed. The above restriction is equivalent to hypothesizing that regulation is ineffective, since it restricts all coefficients of the allowed rate of return s in the system equation 9.10 to zero. The test procedure involves a likelihood ratio test for the restricted and unrestricted forms of the nonlinear system of equations. In addition, Cowing's methodology permits the retrieval of estimated Lagrange multipliers for each observation in the sample. Thus, in addition to the likelihood ratio test for general regulatory effectiveness, it is possible to test for effective regulation (that is, the null hypothesis $\lambda_i = 0$) for each firm in the sample.

The data for Cowing's study are taken from 114 steam-electric plants constructed between 1947 and 1965. The statistical results indicate that rate-of-return regulation is generally effective and exhibits considerable variability in effectiveness across firms and over time.

The study by Hayashi and Trapani is based on an analysis of the comparative static properties of the Averch-Johnson model. These properties, first suggested by McNicol (1973), are found in the derived demand equations of the regulated firm; they are of empirical interest because they are not identical to the analogous comparative statics of the unregulated firm. Denoting, as usual, the capital and labor inputs by K and L with respective prices P_K and P_L and denoting the allowed rate of return by s, McNicol's derived results may be summarized:

$$\frac{\partial K}{\partial P_L} < 0 \quad \frac{\partial K}{\partial P_K} = 0 \quad \frac{\partial K}{\partial s} < 0$$

$$\frac{\partial L}{\partial P_L} > 0 \quad \frac{\partial L}{\partial P_K} = 0 \quad \frac{\partial L}{\partial s} > 0 \tag{9.11}$$

A test for regulatory effectiveness may be carried out by confirming results (equation 9.11) through estimation of the derived demand equations for the regulated firm. A simple extension of McNicol's results leads Hayashi and Trapani to analogous results for the firm's profit-maximizing capital-labor ratio. These results are examined in estimated capital-labor equations for the Cobb-Douglas specification

$$K/L = \alpha_0 + \alpha_1 (P_L/P_K) + \alpha_2 t + \alpha_3 Q + \alpha_4 s$$

and the constraint elasticity of substitution (CES) specification

$$\ln(K/L) = \beta_0 + \beta_1 \ln(P_L/P_K) + \beta_2 t + \beta_3 Q + \beta_4 s$$

where all symbols are as defined before, with Q denoting output and t denoting an index of technology.

Estimating both functional forms using ordinary least squares and firm-level data for 34 electric utilities from 1965 to 1969, Hayashi and Trapani conclude that the results generally support the hypothesis of regulatory effectiveness, and hence overcapitaliza-tion, for the sample period.

The most recent of the empirical studies is by Boyes; this paper is alone among those thus far presented in refuting the existence of the Averch-Johnson thesis. Boyes postulates a "regulated"

profit-maximizing model and a four-input constant ratio of elasticity
of substitution (CRES) production function

$$Q = [\alpha_K K\beta + \alpha_L \; \gamma + \alpha_M M\delta + \alpha_F F\epsilon]^{-(1/\rho)} \; x \; e^u$$

where, in addition to the usual inputs, M represents maintenance; u
is a random disturbance term.[3] The resulting derived demand
equation for capital is shown to contain λ, the Lagrange multiplier
associated with the regulatory constraint:

$$\ln K = [1/ (1+\beta)] \; \ln(\alpha_K \beta/\rho) + [(1+\rho)/(1+\beta)] \; \ln Q$$

$$- [1/ (1+\beta)] \; \ln(r/R' - \lambda(s-r)/(1-\lambda)R') \tag{9.12}$$

where r is the unit price of capital and R' denotes the derivative of
the revenue function with respect to output. Boyes obtains an estimate of λ by estimating equation 9.12 together with the derived demand equations for maintenance, labor, and fuel (which do not contain λ). A likelihood ratio test is used to determine whether λ is
significantly different from zero. Estimating the set of equations for
a sample of 60 steam-electric plants placed in operation between
1957 and 1964, Boyes finds that the likelihood ratio test does not
lead to rejection of the hypothesis $\lambda = 0$; he concludes that the evidence is not supportive of the Averch-Johnson thesis.

In summary, previous studies employing a variety of production structures and testing procedures have generally concluded that
the evidence supports the existence of effective regulation and overcapitalization in the electric utility industry.

Concern with the effects of utility regulation has provided the
impetus for numerous other studies focusing in aspects of the problem which are not considered in this chapter. Stigler and Friedland
(1962), in a study of early attempts at regulation, conclude that the
price of electricity was not significantly affected by regulation.
Westfield (1965) argues that regulation induces utilities to acquiesce
to higher prices on new capital equipment. More recently a study
by Moore (1970) is an attempt to test for the effectiveness of regulation by means of comparing input choices of investor-owned and
public utilities. This requires the assumption that public firms ad-
here to optimization procedures identical to those of private firms.
Such an assumption is difficult to accept on an a priori basis, and
its verification is deemed beyond the scope of the present study;
hence the Moore study does not receive direct consideration in the
literature currently under review. Joskow (1974) constructs a
model which assumes that the behavior of regulatory commissions
is directed primarily at preventing increases in nominal electricity

rates. Thus any nominal rate of return is permitted so long as the firm does not request a rate increase. On the basis of this model Joskow argues that utility regulation is effective.

Since these studies are not directly relevant to the questions currently under investigation, they are not included in the critical survey which occupies the following sections. Instead the present study focuses on the Averch-Johnson model as outlined in the previous section.

MEASURES OF RENTAL PRICE OF CAPITAL

The capital-intensive nature of power generation, together with the nature of rate-of-return regulation, places the unit price of productive capital in a role of fundamental importance for an empirical analysis of regulatory effects. Before discussing the measures which have been employed in previous studies it is worthwhile to describe the essential components of the rental price (or "user cost") of capital as it commonly appears in the investment literature.

$$P_K = B \left(\frac{r(1 - tw)}{(1 - t)} + \frac{d(1 - tv)}{(1 - t)} \right) \qquad (9.13)$$

where B is a measure of equipment costs; r is the "cost of capital"; d is the rate of depreciation on capital equipment; t is the tax rate on corporate income; w is the proportion of total capital service charges deductible as interest for tax purposes; and v represents the proportion of replacement investment deductible as depreciation.[4]

It is seen that the "cost of capital," defined as the minimum prospective yield expected by the firm's current owners on future investment projects, is imbedded in the capital rental price.[5] Since the other components of the rental price may be measured without systematic error, it is the cost of capital which creates potential for measurement error.

In the absence of market risk the cost of capital may be measured by the prevailing rate of interest. In a world of less-than-perfect certainty, however, there arises a broad spectrum of securities of varying yields and degrees of risk. In such a case the firm's cost of capital is no longer a directly observable magnitude, but rather must be inferred from the values which its various securities command in the market. Under these circumstances it is not sufficient to infer the cost of capital solely from yields on less-risky securities such as bonds, for this implicitly assumes that all changes in investors' assessments of market risk will be

reflected in uniform changes in required yields for all classes of
securities. There is little basis for presuming that capital markets
behave in such an orderly fashion, even in so "predictable" a case
as the electric utility industry.

In the following discussion it is contended that the capital
rental prices employed in previous studies share the common shortcoming of reliance on relatively "less risky" security yields as
cost-of-capital measures. In addition, questions are raised concerning the manner in which previous authors have measured other
components of the rental price; indeed, two of the studies under
discussion make no distinction between the rental price and the cost
of capital. In any case failure to measure the rental price without
systematic error leads to doubts about the validity of previous empirical results.

The capital rental price adopted by Boyes (1976) is equivalent
to equation 9.13. The cost of capital, r, is measured by the average yield on Moody's AAA bonds for each year of observation. The
author justifies this measure by citing the annual cost of capital
estimates obtained by Miller and Modigliani (1966), which were
found to conform to changes in Moody's bond yields. It should be
pointed out, however, that the Miller-Modigliani analysis involved
a discontinuous period of only three years (1954, 1956, and 1957),
a dangerously small sample from which to draw inferences about
the general conformity between bond yields and the cost of capital.
Moreover, there is little reason to believe that the conformity found
by Miller and Modigliani can be extrapolated to other periods of
time. It is likely that the 1954-57 period was one in which both
series responded in similar fashion to supply and demand forces
which pervaded capital markets in general. In extending the Miller-
Modigʻ ani results to other periods of time, one must admit the
possibility of changes in the tastes of investors with respect to
risk-bearing or in their collective perception of market risk for
the electric utility industry. As pointed out above, there is little
justification for presuming that the resulting reassessment of the
market values of utility bonds and stocks will be reflected in uniform
changes in their respective required yields. Consequently it cannot
be expected that changes in the cost of capital will be consonant with
changes in bond yields during all periods of time.[6]

An additional criticism of the rental price used by Boyes cen-
ters around his assumption that certain of its other components are
constant across firms. In terms of definition (equation 9.13), it is
assumed that d, v, B, and t are constant for any cross section;
thus the only component of the rental price which is allowed to vary
is w, the proportion of replacement investment deductible as depreciation for tax purposes. As a result, a significant portion of the

variability in the rental price is assumed away and effectively im-
pounded into its regression coefficient in the estimating equations.[7]
This procedure is not necessary, since available annual data make
it possible to reasonably approximate, at the level of the firm, the
various components of the rental price.

Courville (1974) defines the rental price of capital for each
plant as

$$P_K = r \times CF \times B$$

where r is the cost of capital, measured as the yield on Moody's
AAA bonds for the year preceding the initial year of plant operation;
CF is the "capital recovery factor," defined as the uniform annual
payment for an annuity of 40 years' equivalent (at an interest rate r)
to an initial outlay of one dollar; and B denotes the book value of
productive plant.[8]

The use of Moody's average yield lends itself to the same criticism directed previously to the measure used by Boyes. In addition, Courville's measure does not allow for interfirm differences
in depreciation and ignores differences in tax treatments of interest
and depreciation; only the book value of plant is permitted to vary
within a cross section. While the manner in which P_K is measured
does not affect Courville's regression results, it nonetheless plays
a vital role in his test of hypothesis, since the essence of the test
is a comparison of the ratio of marginal products of capital and
labor with the ratio of their prices.

Petersen (1975) adopts the conventional definition of rental
price:

$$P_K = B(r + d - dB/dt)$$

where B, r, and d measure as before the cost of equipment, cost of
capital, and depreciation, respectively, and dB/dt represents the
rate of change of equipment prices (presumably an index of capital
gains on the disposal of equipment); differences in tax treatment are
ignored. The firm's cost of capital is permitted to vary according
to the rating of its bonds. The specific measure chosen is the average yield for bonds in the firm's rating class.[9] Since Petersen
assumes that depreciation and equipment price changes are constant across firms, he arrives at a measure of capital rental price
which varies in a cross section only according to changes in bond
ratings and equipment costs.

The measures adopted by Cowing (1975) and Hayashi and
Trapani (1976) share two defects. First, both fail to distinguish
between the rental price of capital and the cost of capital, and

second, both measure the cost of capital (hence the rental price) by the interest rate on the firm's bond issue immediately preceding the period of observation.

Ignoring the distinction between the cost of capital and the rental price of capital tacitly assumes that equipment costs, depreciation, and tax treatments are constant across firms and over time. This assumption is tenuous at best, particularly as it regards the cost of productive equipment. Measuring the firm's cost of capital by the interest rate on recent debt issues offers the advantage of a measure which is specific to each firm in the sample. However, the use of yield on less-risky securities invites criticisms similar to those addressed to the previously discussed measures. Moreover, the common practice of using a single cost-of-capital measure for all electric utilities in a given cross section is defensible in view of available evidence (for years preceding 1973) and the prevailing consensus of industry observers.[10] Thus it is doubtful whether substantial improvements result from the use of firm-specific cost-of-capital measures; in any case failure to recognize the remaining components of capital rental price casts some doubt on the validity of the measures employed in these two papers.

The final rental price measure for discussion, used by Spann (1974), is equivalent to equation 9.13:

$$P_K = B \left(\frac{r(1 - tw)}{(1 - t)} + d \right)$$

where all symbols are as defined before.[11] Since it is assumed that r, d, t, and w are constant across firms, only the cost of equipment is permitted to vary in any cross section of observations. In this respect Spann's measure warrants criticisms similar to those pertaining to previously discussed measures. In addition, his cost-of-capital measure deserves special attention. The measure chosen is $r = .056$, taken from estimates by Litzenberger and Rao (1971). It should be noted that Litzenberger and Rao, using a valuation model for electric utility shares, drew their sample from the period 1960–66, while Spann's sample is taken from the years 1959–63. The fact that these are overlapping periods is not in itself sufficient justification for assuming that the Litzenberger-Rao results may be applied to the 1959–63 period. In addition, Spann uses this measure for each of the years in his sample; this implicitly assumes that conditions of market risk as perceived by investors were unchanging during this period. There is little evidence to support this hypothesis.

The arguments advanced in this section suggest that there are two grounds on which the capital rental prices of previous studies

may be criticized. On one hand these measures have been unduly
oversimplified through the restriction of various components of the
rental price to constant values; on the other hand the measures generally exhibit a reliance on bond yields as measures of the cost of
capital. With respect to the first problem, a simple expedient suggests itself: More detailed data are available by firm and these may
be utilized to attain superior measurement. With respect to the
second point, it should first be recognized that for purposes of empirical analysis the fundamental issue is whether there exists a
stable positive relationship between bond yields and the cost of capital. If such a relationship exists, then empirical needs are sufficiently well served by the use of yields on bonds. It is the conten-
tion of this chapter, however, that such a relationship may not exist
at every point in time. In particular, circumstances affecting the
electric utility industry which evolved during 1968-72 resulted in
uncertainties which may have disrupted existing relationships between yields on different classes of securities. During this period
there was a growing concern about inflation, particularly with respect to rising prices of increasingly scarce fuels. This period
also witnessed the burgeoning consumer and environmental movements, resulting in legislation directed in part at the electric utility
industry. It is likely that these changes induced investors to re-
assess the earning potential of the industry; and it is unlikely that
the resulting adjustment in required yields was uniform across all
classes of securities.

EMPIRICAL METHODOLOGIES AND
ECONOMETRIC SPECIFICATION

It was noted in the section entitled "Empirical Tests of the
Averch-Johnson Hypothesis" that the studies under discussion have
employed a variety of procedures to test for regulatory effectiveness. The purpose of this section is to elucidate their major short-
comings and to suggest possible improvements in methodology.

The first studies for consideration are those by Spann (1974)
and Boyes (1976). It will be recalled that in each case the testing
procedure involves estimation of the Lagrange multiplier associated
with the firm's regulatory constraint. In Spann's model the Lagrange
multiplier is isolated in a revenue-share equation for capital, while
in Boyes's model it is shown to appear in the firm's demand equation for productive capital. The basic objection to this procedure is
that the Lagrange multiplier is not a parameter to be estimated but
rather a variable quantity across firms in the sample. Although
strictly speaking the Langrange multiplier is not chosen by the firm

in its attempts to maximize profits, it is nonetheless determined simultaneously with the choice variables in the model. Failure to treat it in this manner constitutes an error of specification and produces results of questionable validity.

In addition, the model used in each study rests on restrictive assumptions which could be eliminated by the use of alternative testing procedures. The capital demand equation estimated by Boyes includes the derivative with respect to output of the firm's revenue function.[12] This necessitates a restriction on the revenue function; although Boyes does not discuss this point, presumably the necessary restriction is that the derivative of the revenue function (marginal revenue) is positive for all levels of output. But since the position of an electric utility approximates that of a monopolist, this restriction is equivalent to assuming that the firm's demand curve is price-elastic for all levels of output. It is unlikely that this is the general experience of firms in the electric power industry.

The revenue-share equation estimated by Spann[13] depends critically on the assumption that the firm's demand curve exhibits constant price elasticity of demand. But this class of demand functions includes a special case, that in which demand is represented by a rectangular hyperbola, which is troublesome for Spann's model. In this case total revenue is constant and hence marginal revenue is zero for all levels of output. It is easy to show that a monopolist producing under these conditions maximizes profits by producing an infinitesimal amount of output, a result clearly incompatible with conditions in the electric power industry.

As a final point on the Spann study, it should be noted that the revenue-share equation for capital includes as explanatory variables the levels of factor inputs. But these are endogenous variables in the profit-maximizing model, and Spann's failure to estimate the share equation as part of a larger system of equations explaining input choices is likely to induce simultaneous equation bias in the estimates. Thus the results of his single-equation estimation are subject to question.

The model developed by Courville (1974) involves single-equation estimation of a modified Cobb-Douglas production function. The most important objection is that the model, like that of Spann, includes endogenous variables (factor inputs) as explanatory variables in a single-equation context; but recent developments in the estimation of Cobb-Douglas production functions have generally followed Marschak and Andrews (1944) in specifying that the production function disturbance is "transmitted" to the factor inputs, so that the inputs are not independent of the disturbance.[14] The proper procedure would entail estimation of the production function as one of a system of equations explaining the level of output and the optimal input mix. As Mundlak and Hoch (1965) have shown, ordinary least-squares estimates of this system are consistent only under certain restrictive assumptions regarding the variances and covariances of all the disturbances in the system. In any case Courville's procedure does not reflect the current state of the art in production function estimation, and it is unlikely that his results are free of simultaneous equation bias. Furthermore, problems of simultaneity are aggravated by the use of a capacity utilization measure, that is, the ratio of output to capacity, which leaves the model with the stochastic variable output on both sides of the equation.

An additional problem with Courville's model is that it does not explicitly include regulatory variables; thus the parameter estimates are likely to reflect specification bias in the presence of an effective regulatory constraint. These points taken together cast doubts on the reliability of Courville's estimates as well as his test for overcapitalization.

The basic problem with the study by Hayashi and Trapani (1976) is that the capital-labor ratio equations do not include the price of fuel. This reflects the authors' assumption that the firm's choice of capital and labor is independent of the price of fuel. In view of numerous studies which have elicited evidence of capital-fuel substitution in electric power generation,[15] this constitutes a specification error of considerable proportions, and it undermines the validity of the test for regulatory effectiveness.

The cost-function specification used by Petersen (1975) represents an improvement over those of the previously discussed studies; however, the model is not specified in a manner which is fully consistent with the Averch–Johnson model of the regulated firm. In Petersen's specification the regulatory variable is the difference between the allowed rate of return and the cost of capital.[16] The appropriate specification for the cost function permits the allowed rate of return to enter directly as the regulatory variable. The specification used by Petersen requires an additional assumption, that is, that the procedure followed by regulatory commissions is to maintain a prescribed difference between the allowed rate of return and the cost of capital. This proposition does not follow from the Averch–Johnson model.[17]

In addition, Petersen could have improved the efficiency of his estimates by including in the model the input cost–share equations and estimating these together with the cost function as a set of equations. The information contributed by the share equations would result in more efficient estimates.

The testing procedure adopted by Cowing (1975) is an improvement over the previous studies, but the assumptions implicit in his profit-function specification are more restrictive than those required by alternative specifications.

In particular, the profit-function specification requires the assumption that the firm's output price is exogenous. It is not clear how the problem of rate structure may be confronted in the presence of this assumption. Specifically, as Baumol and Bradford (1970) have pointed out, the profit-maximizing firm subject to a rate-of-return constraint should satisfy that constraint by setting prices in separable markets such that the percentage deviation of price from marginal cost in each market is inversely proportional to the elasticity of demand in that market. Therefore it is necessary that a model such as that used by Cowing, which relies on the assumption that output price is exogenous, should include a mechanism to deal with the possibility that electric utilities (together with their regulatory commissions) may engage in price discrimination in order to generate sufficient revenue to recover total cost or to restrict total revenue in keeping with the profit constraint. Cowing chooses to ignore the problem and thus implicitly assumes that rate structure is constant across firms in his sample. This assumption, however, is not supported by evidence assimilated by Kafoglis and Needy (1975) in a study using 1970 data for privately owned electric utilities. Employing computed Gini coefficients[18] as measures of the "spread" of utility rate structures, the authors demonstrate that there is considerable variability of rate structures in the electric power industry. The issue is further complicated by the use of pricing schemes within each consumer class which relate marginal prices to the level of power consumption. In any case the problem of rate structure introduces into Cowing's model a number of difficulties which must be resolved if the normalized profit function specification is to be retained.

In addition, Cowing's use of profit functions with plant-level data presents the minor problem of measurement of profits at the plant level. Published data on profit contributions by plant are not available, and without such information it is not clear how profits may be accurately imputed to each plant.

CONCLUSION

This chapter gives a critical review of the empirical tests of the Averch–Johnson hypothesis. The tests have been found defective in the measurement of the cost of capital as well as in the assumptions made in the empirical implementation of the tests.

NOTES

1. The interested reader is referred to Baumol and Klevorick (1970).

2. Hotelling's Lemma states that, given the well-behaved profit function $P = P(q,w)$ where q is output and w is the n-dimensional vector of factor prices, the profit-maximizing amount of input i is found by

$$\partial P(q,w)/\partial w_i = P_i(q,w), \; i = 1, \ldots, n.$$

3. It should be noted that the above production function is a special case of the generalized form suggested by Hanoch (1975):

$$\Sigma D_i q^{-e_i d_i} x_i d_i = 1$$

where q is output; x_i is the amount of factor i; D_i, e_i, and d_i are parameters. Setting $e_i d_i$ equal to a constant for all i gives the CRES production function. The Cobb-Douglas and CES forms are also special cases.

4. The definition used in this chapter is taken from Jorgenson (1963). It is presumed that net capital gains on the disposal of equipment are negligible.

5. Throughout this chapter the symbol P_K is referred to as the rental price of capital, reserving for r the phrase "cost of capital."

6. Miller and Modigliani do not suggest that conformity should generally be observed. On the contrary, they remark that the results of their estimation may be due in part to circumstances peculiar to their sample period; see Miller and Modigliani (1966), p. 380.

7. See equation 9.12.

8. It is assumed that the average life of equipment is 40 years.

9. The ratings and average yields are taken from Moody's publications. It should be mentioned that the information in the above discussion does not appear in the published version of Petersen's paper. The cooperation of Petersen in providing the information, as well as other helpful comments, is gratefully acknowledged.

10. See, for example, McDonald (1971) and Myers (1972). The underlying assumption is that electric utilities comprise a "risk-equivalent class."

11. Note that Spann's measure differs from equation 9.13 but only in his implicit assumption that v, the proportion of total replacement deductible as depreciation, is unity. An examination of firm data indicates that this proportion, usually measured as the

ratio of depreciation on the income statement to total replacement, is in fact close to unity and does not vary markedly across firms.

    12. See equation 9.12.

    13. See equation 9.7.

    14. For an elaboration on this point, see Hoch (1958) or Walters (1963). Further refinements are found in Zellner, Kmenta, and Dréze (1966).

    15. See, for example, Dhrymes and Kurz (1964).

    16. See equation 9.9.

    17. Cowing (1975) has pointed out that this specification implicitly assumes that the coefficients associated with the allowed rate of return and the cost of capital are of equal absolute magnitude, a restriction which does not follow from the Averch–Johnson model. Numerous helpful comments and suggestions from Cowing are appreciated.

    18. Previous applications of Gini coefficients have been in the areas of income distribution and industrial concentration.

REFERENCES

Averch, H. and L. L. Johnson. 1962. "Behavior of the Firm under Regulatory Constraint." American Economic Review 52 (December): 1052–69.

Baumol, W., and D. Bradford. 1970. "Optimal Departures from Marginal Cost Pricing." American Economic Review 60, no. 3 (June): 265–83.

Baumol, W., and A. Klevorick. 1970. "Input Choice and Rate of Return Regulation: An Overview of the Discussion." Bell Journal of Economics and Management Science 1 (Autumn): 162–90.

Boyes, W. J. 1976. "An Empirical Examination of the Averch–Johnson Effect." Economic Inquiry 14 (March): 25–35.

Courville, L. 1974. "Regulation and Efficiency in the Electric Utility Industry." Bell Journal of Economics and Management Science 5 (Spring): 53–74.

Cowing, T. G. 1975. "Profit Functions and the Estimation of Regulatory Effectiveness." Presented at the winter meetings of the Econometric Society, Dallas, December 28–30.

Dhrymes, P. J., and M. Kurz. 1964. "Technology and Scale in Electricity Generation." Econometrica 32 (July): 278-315.

Hanoch, G. 1975. "Production and Demand Models with Direct or Indirect Implicit Additivity." Econometrica 43, no. 3 (May): 395-419.

Hayashi, P. M., and J. M. Trapani. 1976. "Rate of Return Regulation and the Regulated Firm's Choice of Capital-Labor Ratio: Further Empirical Evidence on the Averch-Johnson Model." Southern Economic Journal 42, no. 3 (January): 384-98.

Hoch, I. 1958. "Simultaneous Equation Bias in the Context of the Cobb-Douglas Production Function." Econometrica 26: 566-78.

Jorgenson, D. W. 1963. "Capital Theory and Investment Behavior." American Economic Review 53, no. 2 (May): 247-59.

Joskow, P. 1974. "Inflation and Environmental Concern: Structural Change in the Process of Public Utility Price Regulation." Journal of Law and Economics 17 (October): 291-327.

Kafoglis, M., and C. Needy. 1975. "'Spread' in Electric Utility Rate Structures." Bell Journal of Economics and Management Science 6, no. 1 (Spring): 377-87.

Litzenberger, R., and C. Rao. 1971. "Estimates of the Marginal Rate of Time Preference and Average Risk Aversion of Investors in Electric Utility Shares: 1960-66." Bell Journal of Economics and Management Science 1 (Spring): 265-77.

Marschak, J., and W. H. Andrews. 1944. "Randon Simultaneous Equations and the Theory of Production." Econometrica 12 (1944): 143-205.

McDonald, J. G. 1971. "Required Return on Public Utility Equities: A National and Regional Analysis: 1958-1969." Bell Journal of Economics and Management Science 2, no. 1 (Autumn): 503-14.

McNicol, D. L. 1973. "The Comparative Static Properties of the Theory of the Regulated Firm." Bell Journal of Economics and Management Science, Autumn, pp. 428-53.

Miller, M., and F. Modigliani. 1966. "Some Estimates of the Cost of Capital to the Electric Utility Industry, 1954-57." American Economic Review 56 (June): 333-91.

Moore, T. 1970. "The Effectiveness of Regulation of Electric Utility Prices." Southern Economic Journal 36, no. 4 (April): 365–75.

Mundlak, Y., and I. Hoch. 1965. "Consequences of Alternative Specifications in Estimation of Cobb–Douglas Production Functions." Econometrica 33, no. 4 (October): 814–28.

Myers, S. C. 1972. "The Application of Finance Theory to Public Utility Rate Cases." Bell Journal of Economics and Management Science 3 (Spring): 58–97.

Peterson, H. C. 1975. "An Empirical Test of Regulatory Effects." Bell Journal of Economics and Management Science 6 (Spring): 111–26.

Spann, R. M. 1974. "Rate of Return Regulation and Efficiency in Production: An Empirical Test of the Averch–Johnson Thesis." Bell Journal of Economics and Management Science 5 (Spring): 38–52.

Stigler, G., and C. Friedland. 1962. "What Can Regulators Regulate: The Case of Electricity." Journal of Law and Economics 5, no. 2 (October).

Walters, A. A. 1963. "Production and Cost Functions: An Econometric Survey." Econometrica 31, nos. 1–2 (January–April): 1–63.

Westfield, F. 1965. "Regulation and Conspiracy." American Economic Review 55, no. 3 (June): 424–43.

Zellner, A., J. Kmenta, and J. Dréze. 1966. "Specification and Estimation of Cobb–Douglas Production Function Models." Econometrica 34, no. 4 (October): 784–95.

ABOUT THE EDITORS AND CONTRIBUTORS

G. S. MADDALA is graduate research professor in economics, University of Florida. He received his Ph.D. from the University of Chicago.

WEN S. CHERN is an economist in the energy division of the Oak Ridge National Laboratory, Oak Ridge, Tennessee. He received his Ph.D. from the University of California, Berkeley.

GURMUKH S. GILL is supervisory economist, Office of Energy Conservation at the Federal Energy Administration. Before joining the FEA he was an economist in the energy division of the Oak Ridge National Laboratory. He received his Ph.D. from the University of California, Berkeley.

STEVE M. COHN is a computer programmer in the energy division of the Oak Ridge National Laboratory and a graduate student at the University of Tennessee.

WILLIAM W. LIN is an economist in the Economic Research Service, U.S. Department of Agriculture. Prior to joining USDA, he was an economist in the energy division of the Oak Ridge National Laboratory. He received his Ph.D. from the University of California, Davis.

R. BLAINE ROBERTS is associate professor of economics, University of Florida. He received his Ph.D. from Iowa State University.

MICHAEL A. ZIMMER is assistant professor of economics, University of Evansville. He received his Ph.D. from the University of Tennessee.

THE DYNAMICS OF ELECTRICAL ENERGY
SUPPLY AND DEMAND: An Economic Analysis
R. K. Pachauri

THE ECONOMICS OF NUCLEAR AND COAL POWER
Saunders Miller

ENERGY USE AND CONSERVATION INCENTIVES:
A Study of the Southwestern United States
William H. Cunningham
Sally Cook Lopreato

ENVIRONMENTAL REGULATION AND THE
ALLOCATION OF COAL: A Regional Analysis
Alan M. Schlottmann

FINANCING THE GROWTH OF ELECTRIC
UTILITIES
David L. Scott

GEOTHERMAL ENERGY IN THE WESTERN UNITED
STATES: Innovation versus Monopoly
Sheldon L. Bierman
David F. Stover
Paul A. Nelson
William J. Lamont